ENCYCLOPAEDIA OF INDIAN GOVERNMENT: PROGRAMMES AND POLICIES

ENCYCLOPAEDIA
OF
INDIAN GOVERNMENT:
PROGRAMMES AND POLICIES

Vol. 31

Industry: Policies and Development

Edited by

Satish Tiwari

ANMOL PUBLICATIONS PVT. LTD.

NEW DELHI - 110 002 (INDIA)

ANMOL PUBLICATIONS PVT. LTD.
4374/4B, Ansari Road, Daryaganj
New Delhi - 110 002

Encyclopaedia of Indian Government: Programmes and Policies

First Edition, 2000
ISBN 81-261-0515-1 (Set)

PRINTED IN INDIA

Published by J.L. Kumar for Anmol Publications Pvt. Ltd., New Delhi - 110 002 and Printed at Mehra Offset Press, Delhi.

Contents

Preface

Encyclopaedia of Indian Government: Programmes and Policies contains authoritative information on about fifty departmental policies and their future developmental programmes.

Organised to be completed in 40 volumes, this gigantic work covers Agriculture; Atomic Energy; Chemicals and Fertilizers; Coal; Commerce; Communication; Culture; Defence; Education; Environment and Forests; External Affairs; Finance; Food & Consumer Affairs; Food Processing Industries; Health and Family Welfare; Home Affairs and Internal Security; Human Resources; Industry; Information and Broadcasting; Labour; Law, Justice and Company Affairs; Non-conventional Energy Sources; Ocean Development; Parliamentary Affairs; Personnel, Public Grievances and Pensions; Petroleum and Natural Gas; Planning and Programme Implementation; Planning and Statistics; Posts and Telegraphs; Power; Rural Development; Science and Technology; Social Justice and Empowerment; Space; States Affairs; Steel; Steel and Mines; Sugar and Edible Oils; Surface Transport; Textiles; Tourism; Urban Development; Water Resources; Women and Child development etc.

Based on the information derived from authoritative sources, this work contains authentic facts and figures. I am deeply beholden to all the scholars whose writings are cited or substantially made use of in the present work. I am also thankful to Anmol Publications Pvt. Ltd. for undertaking publication of this encyclopaedia. I am solely responsible for shortcomings in presentation of matter.

Encyclopaedic in nature, this will prove a dependable reference work for scholars and academics besides those appearing for different competitive examinations.

—Satish Tiwari

1

Industrial Developments During 1998-99

Department of Industrial Policy & Promotion in the Ministry of Industry is responsible for formulation and implementation of promotional and regulatory measures for sustained growth of the industrial sector, keeping in view the national priorities and socioeconomic objectives.

While the individual Administrative Ministries look after the production, distribution, development and planning aspects of the specific industries allocated to them under the Allocation of Business Rules, 1961, the Department of Industrial Policy & Promotion is responsible for the overall Industrial Policy. Department of Industrial Policy & Promotion also has a number of specific industries allocated to it under the said Rules.

Policy initiatives

The Industrial Policy Resolution of 1956 and the Statement on industrial Policy of 1991, provide the basic framework for the overall Industrial Policy of the Government. Over the years, adjustments have been made in the policy to accelerate the pace of industrial growth by providing greater freedom in investment decisions keeping in view the objectives of efficiency and competitiveness, technological upgradation, maximisation of capacity utilisation and increased exports.

The main objectives of the industrial policy of the Government of India are to reinforce past gains, maintain a sustained growth in productivity, increase gainful employment, ensure optimal utilisation of human resources, attain international competitiveness and transform India into a major partner and player in the global arena. The policy seeks to allow freedom and flexibility to Indian industry in responding to market forces. The Government seeks to provide a policy regime that facilitates and fosters the growth and development of Indian industry. To pursue the aforesaid objectives, Government has been constantly reviewing the policy framework to bring about improvements.

The list of items requiring compulsory licensing is reviewed at regular intervals. During the year under reporting, three industries namely, 'Coal and Lignite', 'Petroleum (other than crude) and its distillation products' and 'Sugar Industry' have been delicensed. Two industries (i.e. Coal and Lignite; and Mineral Oils) for the public sector. Accordingly, barring 6 industries the rest are exempt from licensing. Similarly, there are only four industries reserved for the public sector.

Industries that do not require an Industrial Licence are required to submit an Industrial Entrepreneurs Memorandum to the Secretariat for Industrial Assistance (SIA). For facilitating entrepreneurs, amendments to IEM proposals filed w.e.f 1.7.98 are also being done. Previously, no amendment to IEM was permitted.

In tune with the liberalised Licensing Policy, the Locational Policy has also been significantly amended. There is no requirement of obtaining industrial approvals from the Central Government (except for the industries under compulsory licensing) for locations not falling within 25 kms of cities having a population of more than 1 million. However, notified industries of non- polluting nature such as electronics, computer software and printing may be located within 25 kms of the periphery of cities with more than I million population. Other industries are permitted only if they are located in Industrial Areas designated prior to 25.7.1991. Zoning and Land Use Regulations as well as Environmental Legislation continue to regulate industrial locations.

FDI policy and prospects

The cumulative approval of FDI since 1991 adds up to approximately US $ 46 billion (excluding GDRs) and the total inflows up to December, 1998 are nearly US $ 13.30 billion (excluding GDRs) giving a success rate of around 29%. To bridge the Investment Saving gap (of 3 to 4 percent) in order to achieve a sustained growth of 6 to 7 percent, FDI of the order of US $ 10 billion or more per annum is required. It is in this light that FDI is invited as a measure to supplement domestic efforts, especially because assistance from multilateral and bilateral sources is either stagnant or declining in comparison to private capital flows.

Even in the private capital flows, the short-term foreign capital flows are prone to quick reversal in terms of investors' perception on how the domestic economy is shaping. FDI, which is a long-term investment is, therefore, of crucial importance. FDI is the most desirable form of external funding not only for the long term additional upgradation and modern production and management practices that accompany it.

Recent policy initiatives taken by the present Government are as follows:

— Requirement of prior/final approval by RBI for bringing in foreign investment/allotment of shares against proposals duly approved has been dispensed with. New companies will only have to file the required documents with the RBI regional office within 30 days of issue of shares;

— The Reserve Bank of India has delegated powers to its regional offices for granting Automatic Approval in respect of Foreign Collaboration;

— Foreign Equity up to 100% in the power sector for electric generation, transmission and distribution has been made eligible for automatic approval (barring atomic-reactor plants) provided foreign equity does not exceed Rs. 1500 crore;

— In case of shortfall in NRI contributions in private sector banks, multilateral financial institutions would be allowed to contribute foreign equity to the extent of the shortfall in NRI contributions within the overall limit of 40%;

— Select infrastructure projects of Rs. 100 crore and above are taken up for detailed monitoring to remove bottlenecks and expedite implementation; and

— Two additional activities, namely, "Credit Card Business" and "Money Changing Business" have been included in approved Non Banking Financial activities for FDI and minimum capitalisation norms have been dispensed with, in respect of non-fund based Non Banking Financial activities.

Current industrial performance

The performance of the industrial sector during the current year 1998-99 has not been impressive. The Industrial growth during 1996-97 and 1997-98 was 5.6% and 6.6% respectively as per the Index of Industrial Production (Base 1993-94 = 100). The growth during the current year for the period April-December, 1998 is 3.5% as compared to 6.7% during April-December, 1997.

The analysis of the performance shows that during the nine months of the current year 1998-99 (Apr.-Dec.), under performance is confined to many sectors. The sectors like metal products and parts except machinery and equipment (22.9%), transport equipment and parts (20.8%), paper and paper products (16.0%), beverages, tobacco and related products (13.8%) and rubber, plastic, petroleum and coal products (10.6%) have shown a fairly high growth rate of over 10%.

Positive growth has also been recorded in electricity, food products, basic chemicals & chemical products, leather and fur products, nonmetallic mineral products and wool, silk and man-made fibre textiles. Production has been negative in respect of cotton textiles (-9.9%), manufacture of jute and other vegetable fibre textiles (-5.4%), machinery & equipment other than transport equipment (-3.3%), wood & wood products (-3.3%), textile products (-3.1%) and basic metal & alloy industries (-3.0%).

The overall industrial performance since 1993-94 has been as under:

Sectoral industrial growth %

Base (1993-94 = 100)

Year	Mining (10.47)	Manufacturing (79.36)	Electricity (10.17)	Overall 100.
1993-94	3.5	6.1	7.5	6.0
199495	7.6	8.5	8.5	8.4
1995-96	9.5	13.8	8.1	12.7
1996-97	-1.9	6.7	4.0	5.6
1997-98	5.9	6.7	6.6	6.6
1997-98	5.5	6.9	6.0	6.7
1998-99	-1.1	3.7	6.6	3.5

The slow down in industrial growth can be attributed to both the domestic and external factors. Domestic factors include weak demand on account of inadequate investment in infrastructure sectors such as power, ports and transport, and slow down in general investment mainly due to subdued capital market conditions and partly due to corporate restructuring in some industries in order to become internationally competitive.

The demand has been slackening for basic goods like steel, cement, commercial vehicles, capital goods as well as consumer durables. This has resulted in cut back of production by the industries and buildup of inventories.

On the external side, the export growth has been negative which has been aggravated by fall in world exports. Export growth declined to (-) 2.88% during April-December 1998, following significant deceleration from 21.4% in 1995-96 to 4% in 1996-97 and just 2.6% in 1997-98. As exports constitute 39.7% of total manufacturing output in the country, the decline in exports has adversely affected industrial production.

Investment climate

The investment climate continued to be subdued in 1998-99. The retail investor did not show any inclination for new public issue of equity, forcing corporates to resort to the private placement route. This method of raising resources is gaining importance, because it is both cost and time effective, offers flexibility in structuring, does not require detailed compliance of formalities and need not address retail investors.

The aggregate new capital issues floated by Government Companies, Non-Government Public Limited Companies, Public Sector Undertakings and

Banks and Financial Institutions through prospectus and rights was Rs. 11860 crore in 1997-98 showing a decline of 28.4% compared to 1996-97. The banks and financial institutions also found it difficult to access the capital market through the public and rights issue. The amount raised by the financial intermediaries through this route decreased by 53.7% to Rs. 1632 crore in 1997-98 from Rs. 3579 crore mobilised in the previous year.

In 1997-98, the primary market remained subdued and overall capital raised by new issues is reported to be around Rs. 4, 568 crore. There has been a slight improvement in April-October, 1998 as compared to the corresponding period of last year. The capital raised from the capital market by the corporate sector was Rs. 2689 crore as compared to Rs. 2264 crore in the previous year.

Private placement has emerged as the preferred mode of raising resources by the corporate sector. It recorded an increase of 176.83% in 1997-98 to reach a level of Rs. 27602 crore. The resources raised through private placement accounted for 68.11% of total resources raised, as against 31.02% in 1996-97, Contrary to the earlier years, the banks and the financial institutions raised a major portion of their resources through private placements. In 1997-98, the financial intermediaries raised nearly Rs. 6603 crore through this mode as compared to only Rs. 1925 crore in 1996-97. In fact, nearly 80% of the resources raised by the financial intermediaries was through the private placements.

The number of FIIs registered with the SEBI/ Reserve Bank increased to 496 with a cumulative investment of $ 9283.6 million as on 31st March, 1998. However, the net investment of the FIIs in equity and debt instruments declined during 1997-98 to $ 1649.3 million as compared to $ 2432 million in 1996-97. The subdued conditions have continued in 1998. During

January- September, 19.98 there was a net outflow of $225.2 million.

The secondary market continued to witness volatility. Though the BSE Index at the end of March, 1998 was rather buoyant, movement in share prices exhibited three distinct phases of buoyancy, volatility and generally subdued conditions. However, the price earning ratio declined more sharply from 41.2 in 1994-95 to 19.91 in 1995-96 and further to 15.30 in 1996-97. The PE ratio continues to hover around the same level.

During 1997-98 sanctions of the All India Financial Institutions increased by 49.2% to Rs. 7832 1 crore and disbursement recorded an increase of 28.3% to Rs. 50604 crore. The buoyancy in sanctions and disbursements has continued in 1998-99. For the period April- October of the current financial year, the loan approvals have increased by 39.6% to Rs. 50946.6 crore and the disbursements have increased by 23.3% to Rs. 27248.2 crore as compared to the corresponding period of last year.

Index numbers of wholesale prices

The Wholesale Price Index Numbers are compiled and brought out by the Office of the Economic Adviser on weekly basis. The current series of Wholesale Price Index Numbers (1981-82=100) has been in vogue since July, 1989. Based on the weekly Wholesale Price Index Numbers, monthly and annual Wholesale Price Index Numbers are also compiled. The Office of the Economic Adviser also publishes the monthly Bulletin of Index Numbers of Wholesale Prices in India (1981- 82= 100).

The Wholesale Price Index for all commodities rose from 320.1 during the last week of the financial year 1996-97 (as on 29.3.97) to 337.1 in the last week of 1997-98 (as on 28.3.98) indicating an annual inflation rate of 5.3% compared to 6.9% in 1996-97 (on point to point basis). In the current financial year 1998-99, the WPI (provisional) for the week ending 19.12.98, stood at 355.6 resulting in an annual inflation rate of 6.2% on point to point basis.

A Working Group for the revision of the Current Series of Wholesale Price Index Numbers (1981-82 = 100) was set up in June, 1993 under the Chairmanship of Dr. Y.K. Alagh, formerly Vice-Chancellor, Jawaharlal Nehru University to examine the issues like base year, weighing diagram, commodity coverage, etc. pertaining to the existing series of Wholesale Price Index Numbers (1981-82= 100). Dr. S.R. Hashim, Member-Secretary, Planning Commission is the current Chairman of the Working Group. The Working Group, in order to expedite the work has constituted five subgroups on Agricultural Commodities, Manufactured Items, Unorganised/ Unregistered Industries, Analytical issues and Computerisation. All the subgroups have submitted their respective Reports. 1993-94 has been decided as the base year for the revision of Wholesale Price Index Number Series.

Office of the Economic Adviser in the Ministry of Industry, which is also the Secretariat for the Working Group, is presently in the process of collecting wholesale price information on weekly basis for the period April, 1993 onwards for the commodities/items recommended by the Working Group. Revised WPI series would be compiled and released after the collection price information is completed.

2

Role and Functions

The role and functions of the Department of Industrial Policy and Promotion inter-alia include:-

— Formulation and implementation of industrial policy and strategies for industrial development in conformity with the development needs and national objectives;

— Formulation of Foreign Direct Investment (FDI) Policy and Promotion and approval of FDI;

— Monitoring of the impact of the strategy/policy and its implementation;

— Administration of Industrial (Development & Regulation) Act, 195 1 and rules made thereunder; and

— Advice on all industrial and technical matters.

The Department of Industrial Policy and Promotion, in keeping with the economic policies evolved by the Government, gives direction and takes necessary steps for the development of backward areas, balanced regional development, promotion of FDI, optimum capacity utilization in various sectors of the industry, maximisation of productivity/production, technology adaptation, upgradation and modernization, and improving the international competitiveness of the Indian Industry.

The Department of Industrial Policy and Promotion monitors industrial growth and production in general and in selected industrial sectors, in particular. Appropriate interventions are made on the basis of policy inputs generated by way of monitoring and periodic review of the industrial sector. Besides, the Department assesses and forecasts the need for technological development in specific industrial sector. On this basis, it plans for modernization and technological upgradation of the Indian industry so that, it keeps pace with the international developments in industrial technology on a continuing basis.

Apart from the above, the Department of Industrial Policy and Promotion directly administers a number of important industrial sectors such as automobiles, cement, paper and pulp, industries, machine tools, industrial machinery, engineering industries etc. and is responsible for their development and growth on desired lines.

The Secretariat for the reconstituted Foreign Investment Promotion Board (FIPB) and the Foreign Investment Promotion Council (FIPC) is located in the Deptt. of Industrial Policy & Promotion. The main function of the FIPB is to increase the level of inflow of Foreign Direct Investment (FDI) into the country by providing a time bound transparent and pro-active FDI regime. It is headed by Secretary, Deptt. of Industrial Policy & Promotion. The main function of Foreign Investment Promotion Council (FIPC) is to facilitate foreign direct investment & identification of priority areas etc.

The "Investment Promotion and Infrastructure Development Cell (IP&ID)" constituted to give further impetus to facilitation and monitoring of investment as well as for better coordination of infrostructural requirements for industry has been strengthened to make it more effective. The Cell has been, inter-alia, given the responsibility of dissemination of information about investment climate in India, investment facilitation, monitoring of Industrial Entrepreneur Memorandum (IEM), Letter of Intent (LOI) and Foreign Collobration (FC) approval, coordination of progress of infrastructure sectors approved for investment/technology transfer, promotion of private investment including foreign investment in the infrastructure sector, compilation of sectoral policies, strategies and guidelines of infrastructure sector and facilitating preparation of a perspective plan of infrastructure requirements for industry.

A Project Monitoring Wing has been created within the IP & ID Cell with a view to monitoring implementation of approved projects and for facilitating solution to the investor problems through direct interaction and updation of information on the projects.

A Facilitation Center is already functioning near Gate No. 13, Udyog Bhawan which provides free pamphlets and Promotional Policy literature relating to policy and procedures announced by the Central Government and State Governments to the prospective investors. Dissemination of information about the policy and procedures is also done through internet web site at the following address :-

http: "www.nic.in/indmin

A separate unit called Entrepreneurs Assistance Unit (EAU) is functioning to guide prospective entrepreneurs with respect to licensing policy and procedures, foreign collaboration and import of capital goods etc. This unit also looks after public grievances and complaints. The unit is headed by a Public Relations and Complaints Officer (PR&CO) under the overall charge of a Joint Secretary who has been designated as Joint Secretary

(Establishment and Public Grievances). Complaints relating to monitoring of IEM, LOI and FC approval are to be settled within 10 working days of their receipt. Additional Secretary & Financial Advisor (AS&FA) functions as "Business Ombudsperson" to look into complaints relating to delays in clearance of projects/ approvals. These complaints can be filed either at this unit or at Facilitation Center, IP & ID Cell.

This Department has issued a Citizens' Charter prepared by task force under the Chairmanship of Secretary (IP&P) with a view to achieving excellence in the formulation and implementation of Industrial Policies and providing prompt and efficient services to its clients for smooth implementation and operation of Industrial Projects. According to the Charter the objectives as outlined in the Industries (Development and Regulation) Act i.e. dispersal of industries, development of backward areas, productivity enhancement and judicious resource utilization shall be the guiding principles of the Department.

The Charter also spells out standards for general procedures as well as industrial approvals and promotional measures to assess the Department's performance against these standards and promises to display the results through periodical publications. Implementation of various commitments and standards laid down in the Charter is being closely monitored.

3

Evolution and Development

Main features of industrial policy

The main objectives of the industrial policy of the Government of India are to reinforce past benefits, maintain sustained growth in productivity, increase gainful employment, achieve optimal utilisation of human resources, attain international competitiveness and transform India into a major partner and player in the global arena.

The policy seeks to deregulate Indian industry so as to allow it freedom and flexibility in responding to market forces. The Government seeks to provide a policy regime that facilitates and fosters growth and development of Indian industry.

To pursue the aforesaid objectives, Government has been constantly reviewing the policy framework to bring it in alignment with global practices. Some of the important policy measures announced and procedural simplifications undertaken are as follows-.-

Industrial licensing

The list of items requiring compulsory licensing is constantly reviewed. During the year under reporting, three industries, namely, Coal and Lignite, Petroleum (other than crude) and its distillation products and Sugar Industry have been delicensed. Two industries (i.e. Coal and Lignite; and Mineral Oils) have been taken out from the list of industries reserved for the public sector. Accordingly, now only six industries are under compulsory licensing mainly on account of environmental, safety and strategic considerations. Similarly, there are only four industries reserved for the public sector.

Industrial entrepreneur's memorandum (IEM)

Industries not falling under licensing are required to only submit an Industrial Entrepreneurs Memorandum (IEM) to the Secretariat for Industrial Assistance (SIA). No industrial approval is required for such exempted industries. For facilitating entrepreneurs, amendments to IEM proposals filed w.e.f. 1.7.98 are also being done. Previously, no amendment to TEM was permitted.

Locational policy

In tune with the liberalised Licensing Policy, the Locational Policy has also been significantly amended. There is no requirement of obtaining industrial approvals from the Central Government (except for the industries under compulsory licensing) for locations not falling within 25 Kms of cities having a population of more than I million. Notified industries of non-polluting nature such as electronics, computer software and printing may be located within 25 Kms of the periphery of cities with more than 1 million population. Other industries are permitted only if they are located in Industrial Areas designated prior to 25.7.1991. Zoning and Land Use Regulations as well as Environmental Legislation continue to regulate industrial locations.

Policy for small scale industries

The Government continues to provide protection to the small scale sector, inter alia, through the policy of reserving items for exclusive manufacture in the small scale sector. 8 12 items are reserved for manufacture in this sector. Investment limits on plant and machinery for small scale and ancillary industrial undertakings have been increased to Rs 3 crore. All industrial undertakings, other than the small scale industrial undertakings engaged in the manufacture of items reserved for exclusive manufacture in the small scale sector are required to obtain an industrial licence and undertake an export obligation of 50 percent of the annual production.

Investment promotion & infrastructure development

This Cell has been functioning in the Department of Industrial Policy and Promotion for the last two years for purposes of dissemination of information, investment facilitation, and coordination of progress made in infrastructure projects. The following activities have been undertaken by the Cell during the period of this report:-

Project monitoring wing

During the year 1998-99, a Project Monitoring Wing has been set up as part of this Cell to collect and compile information on progress of implementation of approved large projects. This information is obtained through interaction with Central Ministries and State Governments.

100% export oriented units (EOU scheme)

The scheme for 100% Export Oriented Units (EOUs) was introduced in 1980 for generating production capacity for exports. Under this scheme, the units are eligible to procure the machinery, raw materials, components, consumables etc. from indigenous/ imported sources, free of excise/custom duty.

The units are required to export their entire production and achieve a minimum Net Foreign Exchange Earning as a Percentage of exports (NFEP) of 20% or as prescribed for specified sectors. They can sell up to 25% of their production in Domestic Tariff Area (DTA) on payment of applicable duties. In case of Agra based industries, the DTA sale can be allowed up to 50%. The Development Commissioners (DCs) of concerned Export Processing Zones (EPZ) are the authorised agencies to allow DTA sale of production as per the provisions of the Import Export Policy in force, on payment of applicable duties.

Under this scheme, the entrepreneurs can choose the location in accordance with the locational policy of the Govt. and the premises, where the manufacturing activity is to be carried out, are custom-bonded.

100% foreign equity is permissible under the EOU scheme.

For expeditious disposal of the problems faced by entrepreneurs, the Development Commissioners of the Export Processing Zones have been delegated powers to approve several post-approval amendments. During the period under review, the powers of Development Commissioners have been enhanced as follows :

— to approve extension in validity of approval letters by 3 years as against earlier powers to approve extension in validity by one year only; and

— to permit disposal of capital goods (less than 5 years old) in Domestic Tariff Area (DTA) on payment of applicable duties. Earlier, the Development Commissioners could permit disposal of capital goods more than 5 years old in DTA.

During 1. 1.98 to 3 1.12.98, 246 approvals were issued under EOU scheme, to set up projects in various sectors like drugs, chemicals, oil refinery, textiles, electronics etc. These proposals envisage investment on fixed assets to the extent of Rs. 6 196.25 crore, with export turnover of Rs. 5245 1.57 crore during their five year of operation.

The total employment projected in these 246 EOUs is 36594.

Out of the aforesaid 246 approvals for setting up EOUs, 59 EOU proposals were approved with Foreign Collaborations envisaging foreign investment of Rs. 328.51 crore.

EHTP/STP Scheme

For building up strong electronics industry with a view to enhance the export, two schemes, viz. Electronics Hardware Technology Park (EHTP) and Software Technology Park (STP) are In operation. The applications for setting up projects under these schemes, are considered by the Inter-Ministerial Standing Committee (IMSC) chaired by Secretary (Electronics). The IMSC is serviced by the SIA. Under EHTP/STP scheme also, the inputs are allowed to be procured free of duties.

During the period under review, the Directors of STPs have been given powers to approve post- approval amendments in respect of EHTP/STP projects as have been given to the Development Commissioners of Export Processing Zones in case of Export Oriented Units.

Under the EHTP/STP scheme, 63 approvals were issued during 1. 1.98 to 3 1.12.98 envisaging exports worth Rs. 3481.36 crore in five years. In respect of EHTP/STP proposal, foreign investment of Rs. 175.44 crore was approved during this period.

Technical development fund and nonresident Indians

The Government of India announced the New Industrial Policy Statement in 1991 allowing 100% NRI/OCB equity participation in the 34 categories/ groups of High Priority Industries. The list now includes 25 more industries. It has also been decided to permit 100% NRI/OCB investment on full repatriation basis in Export/

Trading/Star Trading Houses at par with High Priority Industries.

NRI/OCBs are also allowed to invest up to 100% services of international standards to the India equity with full benefit of repatriation in industries consumers requiring compulsory licensing and items reserved for Small Scale Industries Sector with necessary export obligation.

100% NRI/OCB equity is also allowed in Hotel and Tourism Related Industries, Hospitals, Advanced Diagnostic Centres, Shipping, Mining, Export Oriented Deep Sea Fishing Industries and Oil Exploration. A decision has also been taken to allow 100% equity participation by NRI/OCBs on repatriation basis in the Real Estate Development and Housing Sector.

NRI/OCBs are allowed to invest in Aviation Sector up to 100% on repatriation basis and up to 40% in the Banking Sector.

Entrepreneurs assistance unit (EAU)

The Entrepreneurs Assistance Unit (EAU) functioning under the SIA provides assistance to prospective entrepreneurs with respect to licensing policy and procedures, foreign collaboration etc. The Unit attends to enquiries from entrepreneurs relating to investment decisions and also provides information regarding status of applications filed for various industrial approvals.

A separate computerised counter called "Information Facilitation Counter" has been set up for attending enquiries/grievances from the members of the public. Information Facilitation Counter is headed by the Public Relations and Complaints Officer (PR&CO) under the overall charge of a Joint Secretary who has been designated as Joint Secretary (Establishment and Public Grievances). The grievances are acknowledged across the counter and a final disposal letter is normally issued within a period of three months. More than 900 entrepreneurs visited the Information Facilitation Counter during the year i.e. fill December, 1998. The counter has received more than 30 enquiries seeking information on status of pending proposals apart from one grievance during this period. All enquiries/grievances were attended to expeditiously.

Foreign investment policy

The measures introduced by the Government to liberalise provisions relating to Foreign Direct Investment (FDI) have been consolidated and further expanded into new areas. The Government is committed to promote increased inflow of FDI and its intended benefits such as better and high technology, modernisation, increased opportunity of exports and providing products and services of international standards to the Indian consumers.

To achieve these objectives, it is the Government's continuing endeavours not only to provide greater transparency in the policy and procedures but to also enable a more dynamic and investor friendly policy framework. With this end in view high priority sectors with 50/51/74/100% foreign equity are already under Automatic Approval Route.

To provide greater transparency to the approval process, the Government has issued a set of guidelines for the consideration of proposals by the Foreign Investment Promotion Board (FIPB) so as to make prospective investors aware of the issues which are up to 100% on repatriation basis and up to 40% in the considered by the FIPB while deciding proposals.

Some of the initiatives taken by the Secretariat for Industrial Assistance (SIA) are:

— In line with the economic reform policy inter alia aimed at deregulation and decontrol of industry, three more industries have been delicensed, namely: (i) Coal & Lignite and Petroleum (other than crude) and its distillation products and (iii) Sugar Industry With this the list of industries requiring compulsory licensing has been reduced to 6 on the basis of environmental, strategic and safety considerations;

— The Ministry has taken up a consultative exercise with Administrative Ministries concerned for bringing in further clarity in the sectoral policies concerning FDI. Foreign Equity up to 1000/'0' in Power Sector for electric generation, transmission and distribution as also roads & highways, ports & harbours, and vehicular tunnels and bridges has been made eligible for automatic approval provided foreign equity does not exceed Rs. 1500 crore,-

— Requirement of prior approval by RBI for bringing in FDI/NRI/OCB investment and issue of shares to foreign investors after FIPB/ Government approval has been done away with. New companies will have to file the required documents with the concerned regional office of the RBI within 30 days of issue of shares. However, they are also required to intimate RBI of receipt of inward remittances within 30 days.

— The Reserve Bank of India has delegated powers to its Regional offices for granting Automatic Approval in respect of Foreign Technical Collaboration (FT);

— As per new procedure, the applications for setting up Export Oriented Units/Units in Export Processing Zones are to be submitted to the Development Commissioner of Export Processing Zones directly would require Foreign Investment Promotion Board/ Government approval and applications for foreign equity are to be routed through SIA.

— The facility available to EOU/EPZ units in regard to automatic approval for payment of lumpsum fee and royalty for foreign technical collaboration have now been made at par with the general facility available to non-EOU/EPZ units i.e., lumpsum fee up to US$ two million and royalty payments up to 8% on exports and 5% on sales /DTA sales over a period of 5 years from the date of commercial production,-

— Development Commissioners have been delegated with powers to permit disposal of obsolete capital goods (used for less than five years) on payment of applicable duties, up to a maximum limit of Rs. 10/- lakh in each financial year for an EOU/EPZ unit; to permit import of office equipment not exceeding 20% of the total capital goods value, subject to EXIM policy up to a maximum limit of Rs. 25/- lakh; and to permit merger of two or more EOU/EPZ units, provided the unit falls within the jurisdiction of the same Development Commissioner and the some Commissioner of Central Excise and Customs,-

— Procedure for filing of Industrial Entrepreneur's Memorandum (IEM) in composite form has also been streamlined. Amendments /Modifications allowed to the Entrepreneurs with reference to the status/ regulations /notifications issued by the Central/ State Governments from time to time;

— Two additional activities namely "Credit Card Business" and "Money Changing Business" have been included in the approved activities of FDI;

— Minimum Capitalisation Norm has been dispensed with in respect of non-fund based NBFC activities;

— Foreign Direct Investment up to 40% by multilateral financial institutions allowed in the case of Private Sector Banks, within the overall limit of 40% for FDI, including NRI Investment,-

— Proposals for manufacture of cigarettes with FDI up to 100% are now allowed. Such approvals shall be subject to the provisions relating to compulsory licensing under the Industries (Development and Regulation) Act, 1951;

— For Foreign Collaboration and Industrial Licence, a revised composite form has been prescribed,-

— To encourage investment by Non Resident Indians (NRIs)/Overseas Corporate Bodies (OCBs) individual NRIs/OCBs can now invest in a listed company up to 5 percent of its equity (up from I percent); the aggregate investment limit for all NRI/OCB investment is to be increased from 5 percent to 10 percent;

— As announced by the Hon'ble Prime Minister, the FIPB is making all efforts to give a firm 'Yes' or 'No' to FDI proposals within a stipulated time frame;

— A Project Monitoring Unit has been set up within the Department to monitor and facilitate smooth implementation of large FDI projects having foreign equity of Rs. 100 crore and above,- and

— Foreign financial /technical collaborators with past/existing joint ventures to seek Foreign Investment Promotion Board /Government approval in case of setting up new joint ventures in the same or allied activities.

4

Foreign Direct Investment

Foreign Direct Investment (FDI) is essential for bridging the Investment-Saving gap to achieve sustained growth. The current level of domestic saving, which is around 26 per cent of GDP, can at best support a GDP growth of 6 per cent. Given an incremental capital output ratio (ICOR) of 4.3, sustained growth at 6 to 7 per cent per annum will require an average investment rate of 27 to 32 per cent. Therefore, domestic saving has not only to be augmented but also supplemented with external resources.

FDI is the most desirable route for bridging this gap, as it is non-debt creating as also not prone to quick reversal unlike portfolio investment. FDI's importance also lies in the fact that assistance from multilateral and bilateral sources is either stagnant or declining in comparison to private capital flows. Further, besides the long-term additional capital it brings in, FDI also facilitates technology upgradation and introduction of modern production and management practices.

Policy

The Government policy on FDI since 1991 has been aimed at encouraging foreign investment, particularly in core and infrastructure sectors. While foreign investment is welcomed in wide-ranging activities, simultaneous measures have also been introduced to ensure a level playing field to the domestic industry and also to protect national interests. These measures, which have been imposed on the basis of sector-specific sensitivities, inter alia include conditions such as dividend balancing, foreign exchange neutrality, export obligation, cap on foreign equity, etc.

Recent policy initiatives taken by the present Government inter alia include simplification of foreign investment procedures; allowing foreign investment in new activities such as Global Mobile Personal Communication Systems; FDI up to 100 per cent in power sector under automatic route; the same facility has now been extended to roads & highways, ports & harbours, vehicular tunnels and vehicular bridges; etc.

Performance

The cumulative approval of FDI since 1991 adds up to approximately US$ 48 billion (excluding GDRs) and the total inflows up to December, 1998 are nearly US$ 13.58 billion (excluding GDRs) giving a success rate of around 28.29%, which, if adjusted to contingency and mutually exclusive approvals in the power, telecom and LNG sectors takes the success rate to nearly 36%. Essentially, low gestation projects such as electrical and electronic equipment, computer software, services and processed foods have registered speedy inflows whereas in the case of capital intensive long gestation projects the inflows have been slower.

During 1998, FDI inflow (excluding GDRs) has been of the order of Rs. 132692. 1 million against Rs. 129892.7 million during 1997. Thus, FDI inflows have not shown any negative trend notwithstanding economic sanctions.

In terms of origin of investment approvals, since 1991, USA accounts for the highest share followed by Mauritius, UK, Japan and Germany.

During the current year, major approvals in terms of investment pertain to USA followed by Belgium, UK, Mauritius and Australia. In terms of number of approvals this year, the ranking is USA followed by Germany, U.K., Japan and Mauritius.

In terms of sectoral distribution of approvals, since 1991, power sector accounts for 2 1 per cent followed by telecommunications (17%) oil refinery (13%), transportation (6%), chemicals other than fertilizers (6%) and services sector (5%).

During the current year up to December 1998, oil refineries account for the major share of investment approved (28%) followed by power (14%), metallurgy (8%), telecommunications (8%) and chemicals (7%). In terms of number of approvals, electrical equipment (including electronics and computer software) ranks first followed by transportation, chemicals, mechanical engineering and industrial machinery.

Since inception, Mauritius has accounted for maximum inflows (19.9%) followed by USA (12.3%), Japan (4.4%), Germany (4.1 %) and UK (3.5%). During the current year also Mauritius ranks first in inflows accounting for 22% of total inflows followed by USA (10.2%), Japan (5.9%), Germany (4.7%) and South Korea (3.3%). During 1998, telecommunications (14%) accounted for major inflows followed by transportation 111 %) chemicals other than fertilizers (8%) and services

NRI investment

The general Policy and facilities for foreign direct investment as available to foreign companies are fully applicable to NRIs as well. In addition, Government have extended some concessions specially for NRIs and OCBs, which include investment in the real estate sector up to 100 per cent.

Proposals envisaging NRI investment of Rs. 74,61 0 million (excluding approvals granted under RBI Schemes) have been approved by the Government from 1991 to December, 1998. NRI inflows have been of the order of Rs. 80,036 million, including NRI schemes approved by RBI, which gives a fairly high success rate and shows the confidence of NRIs in our strong economic fundamentals.

FDI approvals- state-wise

The choice of location of projects depends on the commercial judgement of investors basing on factors such as market size and growth; availability of skilled manpower; availability and dependability of infrastructure facilities; fiscal and other incentives provided by State Governments; etc.

The Central Government supplements State Governments' efforts by providing special incentives for investments in core sector as also high priority industries such as information technology.

States of Maharashtra, Tamil Nadu, Karnataka, Delhi, Andhra Pradesh, Gujarat, Haryana, Uttar Pradesh and West Bengal account for major portion of FDI investments approved so far.

FDI inflows in south, east and south-east Asia

FDI inflows in India have shown a continuous upward trend (53% growth in 1997 as compared to 1996) whereas FDI inflows have more or less remained stagnant or have marginally fallen during the lost 2 - 3 years in countries such as Malaysia, Republic of Korea and Indonesia. In Vietnam FDI inflows have registered a steep decline in 1997(46%).

FDI inflows in Singapore have increased only marginally in 1997 (6%). Though, there has been a perceptible increase in FDI inflows in Thailand in 1997, it is probably on account of the steep currency crisis leading to lower acquisition costs. China is the only country, apart from India, where the FDI inflows have grown continuously.

Prospectus

The advantages of the Indian destination rest on strong fundamentals. A large and growing market- world-class scientific, technical and managerial manpower; abundance of labour and natural resources; independent judiciary etc., add to India's advantage. This is now recognised by a number of global investors and they have either already established a base in India or are in the process of doing so. Ongoing initiatives such as simplifications of legislation, delicencing, setting up regulatory authorities such as Central/State Electricity Regulatory Commissions, etc. will provide the necessary impetus to accommodate enlarged FDI inflows in future.

In the final analysis, large volume of inflows of FDI would depend on domestic economic conditions and the FDI policy, world economic trends, and strategies of global investors. Government, on its part is fully committed to creating strong economic fundamentals and an increasingly proactive FDI policy regime.

5

Analysis of Industrial Approvals

Industrial licence applications

Ever since the announcement of New Industrial Policy (NIP) in July 1991, and delicensing of most of the industries, the number of applications for Industrial licence has been declined. Till December, 1998, 162 applications had been received. The overall pendency in respect of Industrial Licence applications has also come down substantially to 61 by the end of December, 98 from 285 at the end of December, 1997. The following table gives a picture of the disposal of pendency in respect of old as well as fresh applications for industrial licence:-

Status of application for industrial licence	1998 (Jan.-Dec.)	1997
Applications awaiting disposal as on 1.1.98	285	543
Applications received/ registered during the year	162	406
Total number of pending application	447	949
Number of applications disposed of during the year	386	664
Balance pending applications as on 3 1.12.98	61	285

Industrial entrepreneurs memoranda (IEM)

The Industrial Policy has been liberalised in July, 1991, Under the New Industrial Policy, the schemes of Registration of Industries, viz. De-licensed Industries Registration (DLR), Exempted Industries Registration and other technical authorities like Office of the Textile Commissioner and Development Commissioner for Iron & Steel have been abolished.

For all Industries which were registered earlier and those which are de-licensed after the announcement of New Industrial Policy, an entrepreneur has to file an Industrial Entrepreneur Memorandum to the Secretariat for Industrial Assistance (SIA) in the prescribed form.

The receipt of the IEM is computerised and acknowledged immediately by SIA. No further approval is required from this Ministry in respect of de-licensed industries.

IEMs filed with SIA during post liberalisation period

Since the announcement of New Industrial Policy till the end of December, 1998, 35 153 IEMs have been filed with the Government for establishing new units, new articles and for expansion of existing units etc. These IEMs had a proposed investment of about Rs. 653 thousand crore and proposed employment of more than 60 lakh persons.

Since the inception of the IEM scheme, till December, 1998 a total of 3481 Units have formally intimated commencement of commercial production. The actual investment reported in respect of these IEMs is about Rs. 123945 crore.

Foreign direct investment

The Policy initiatives taken have catalysed investment as is evident from the buoyancy in approvals for foreign direct investment:

Year (January December	Approvals involving foreign direct investment	Total foreign direct investment approved (Rs. in million)
19991	289	5341.1
1992	692	38875.4
1993	785	88593.3
1994	1062	141871.9
1995	1355	320717.9
1996	1559	361468.1
1997	1665	548913.5
1998	1191	308135.0
Total	8598	1813915.5

The figures are inclusive of 58 proposals approved by FIPB for Global Depository Receipts (GDRs)/ Foreign Currency Convertible Bonds (FCCBs) amounting to Rs. 19409.82 crore during 1994 to December, 1998.

Foreign Investment approvals during the year 1997 (i.e. January to December 1997), Rs. 548913 million has exceeded the all time high recorded during the full year of 1996 (Rs. 361468 million)

There has generally been an apprehension that foreign investment approvals are not flowing into the desired areas. This is not correct. Analysis indicates that in reality, over 80% of the approvals for foreign investment are in the priority areas. In fact, the sector-wise distribution of approvals of foreign investment is in such important sectors as power, oil refineries, electronics and electrical equipments, chemicals and food processing industries. In addition, foreign investment approvals are significantly high in sectors like telecommunications, transportation, industrial machinery etc. This is evident

Sl. No.	Name of Industry Total	No. of approvals Total	Tech	Fin	Amount of FDI approved	% of total
1.	Power	183	16	167.0	334143.90	18.43
2	Telecommunication (Radio Paging, Cellular Mobile/ Basic Telephone Services	478	109	369.0	327408.50	18.06
3.	Oil Refinery	343	146	197.0	243652.60	13.44
4.	Chemicals (other than Fertilizers)	1364	698	666.0	112301.70	6.19
5.	Service Sector (Financial, Non Financial, Banking & other Services)	590	36	554.0	115695.60	6.38
6.	Metallurgical Industries	539	295	244.0	111496.90	6.15
7.	Transportation Industry (including Automobile)	895	433	462.0	112066.80	6.18
8.	Electrical Equipment (Computer Software & Electronics)	2490	987	1503.0	95155.60	5.25
9.	Food Processing Industries	698	137	561.0	83406.00	4.60
10.	Hotel & Tourism	328	112	216.0	34906.30	1.93
11.	Textile (include dyed, printed	547	114	433.0	28069.10	1.55

12. Miscellaneous Industries (Horticulture Agriculture, Floriculture and other industries)	1159	613	546.0	24871.10	1.37
13. Paper & Pulp Industries	152	62	90.0	23087.60	1.27
14. Industrial Machinery	1161	736	425.0	19584.00	1.08
15. Consultancy Services	424	80	344.0	17082.30	0.94
16. Glass	78	28	50.0	13416.80	0.74
17. Trading	351	16	335.0	12188.30	0.67
18. Fermentation Industry	58	17	41.0	11255.10	0.62
19. Miscellaneous mechanical and engineering industry	580	247	333.0	11200.00	0.62
20. Rubber Goods	170	89	81.0	10574.90	0.58
21. Sugar	7	1	6.0	10007.50	0.55
22. Commercial, Office and Household equipment	70	27	43.0	9817.90	0.54
23. Drugs & Pharmaceuticals	307	171	136.0	8019.80	0.44
24. Ceramics	180	52	128.0	7903.70	0.44
25. Cement & Gypsum Products	79	33	46.0	7026.30	0.39

26. Agricultural Machinery	36	27	9.0	4341.10	0.24
27. Soaps, cosmetics & toilet preparations	48	15	333361.8	0.19	
28. Machine Tools	160	76	84.0	2785.40	0.15
29. Leather, Leather goods and Pickers	163	33	130.0	2742.20	0.15
30. Fertilisers	58	52	6.0	2468.80	0.14
31. Medical and Surgical Appliances	66	24	42.0	2418.20	0.13
32. Photographic raw film and paper	19	10	9.0	2214.50	0.12
33. Vegetable Oils and Vanaspati	35	3	32.0	1939.30	0.11
34. Boilers and steam generating plants	69	40	291.0		
35. Industrial Instruments	157	90	67.0	1165.80	0.06
36. Dyestuffs-	18	3	15.0	1067.20	0.06
37. Earth-moving machinery	50	31	19.0	833.40	0.05
38. Prime movers (other than electrical)	60	38	22.0	913.20	0.05
39. Scientific Instruments	40	14	26.0	614.30	0.03
40. Mathematical, surveying & drawing	5	1	4.0	383.70	0.02
41. Timber products	10	2	8.0	163.20	0.01
42. Defence Industries	5	4	1.0	34.7 0.00	
Grand total	14230	5718	8512.0	1812965.5	100.00

from the following industry-wise break up of foreign collaboration cases approved from 01.08.91 to 31. 12.1998:

The break up of foreign direct investments (FDI) and foreign technology agreements of the major investing countries during 1991-1998 are as follows :

No.	Country	No. of approvals			% to total
		Total	Financial	Technical	technical approved Nos.
1	U.S.A	2896	1560	1336	22.44
2	Germany	1707	834	873	14.66
3	U. K	1451	760	691	11.61
4	Japan	993	395	598	10.05
5	Netherlands	695	433	262	4.40
6	Italy	684	318	366	6.15
7	Switzerland	556	299	257	4.32
8	France	512	272	240	4.03
9	Mauritius	424	399	25	0.42
10	Singapore	416	327	89	1.49
11	Korea(South)	392	235	157	2.64
12	Australia	311	188	123	2.07
13	Canada	195	112	83	1.39
14	Austria	186	73	113	1.90
15	NRI	895	886	9	0.15
16	Other Countries	2238	1507	731	12.28
	Total	14551	8598	5953	100.00

The buoyancy in actual FDI inflow would be evident from the chart below and is indicative of the progress in implementation and of the growing confidence of investors.

The total FDI approved and the actual FDI inflow have been as below :-

Year	FDI Approved	Actual Inflows of FDI
1991	5341.1	3514.3
1992	38875.4	6751.8
1993	88593.3	17867.1
1994	141871.9	32892.8
1995	320717.2	68200.2
1996	361468.1	103892.0
1997	548913.5	164253.3
1998	308135.0	133203.6
Total	1813915.5	530575.1

The approved and actual FDI inflow in respect of major investor countries between January, 1991 to December, 1998 indicates that such inflows have already commenced.

(Rupees in million)

SI. No.	Name of the Country	Approvals 1991-98	Actual inflow 1991-98
1.	U.S.A	426093.1	65430.3
2.	Mauritius	183952.9	105752.6
3.	U. K	130136.7	18319.1
4.	Japan	75129.5	23337.3
5.	Germany	67603.1	21529.3
6.	Korea (South)	60411.7	19263.1
7.	Australia	59062.8	1693.2
8.	Malaysia	54444.7	1322.8
9.	Israel	42270.2	1345.8

10.	Netherlands	40632.9	18151.8
11.	Belgium	39046.8	1983.7
12.	Cayman Island	36218.7	30.0
13.	France	35868.1	7013.5
14.	Singapore	33338.7	10582.1
15.	Italy	26880.5	6638.3
16.	NRIs	74609.6	80036.1
	Total	1813915.5	530575.1

NRI Investment

During the period 1.4.1998 to 31.12.1998, as many as 34 proposals from NRIs were approved.

The details of NRI approvals are as follows :

Letter of Intent	:	Nil
FC Approvals	:	34
Total	:	34

Between the period August, 1991 and December, 1998, NRI/OCB investment of Rs. 6978.00 crore has been approved.

6

Dispersal of Industries

Balanced regional development through locational dispersal of industries has been one of the principal objectives of the successive Five Year Plans. With a view to achieving this objective, the Government has provided several incentives/concessions, including the new Growth Centre Scheme and the Transport Subsidy Scheme. While some of these measures aim at directly assisting the entrepreneurs, others seek to achieve the development of the areas as a whole.

New growth centre scheme

With a view to promoting industrialisation of the backward areas in the country, the Government of India, in June, 1988, had announced the Growth Centre Scheme under which 71 Growth Centres were proposed to be set up throughout the country. Under this scheme, Growth Centres would be provided with basic infrastructure facilities such as power, water, telecommunications and banking, so as to enable them to attract new industries. Growth centres have been allocated amongst States by the Planning Commission on the basis of a combined criteria of population 'in relation to industrial potential and unemployment, area and extent of industrial backwardness.

Each of the selected growth centre is to be developed in an area of about 400-800 hectares at an estimated project cost of about Rs. 25-30 crore, with financial assistance from the Centre and State Governments in the following manner:

1. Centre (Equity) Rs. 10 Crore

2. State (Equity) Rs. 5 Crore

The total amount of Central assistance released under the Scheme since its inception is Rs. 270.27 crore. The year-wise break up is indicated in the table :-

Year	Amount (Rs. in crore)
1990-91	15.00
1991-92	36.50
1992-93	14.74
1993-94	07.00
1994-95	80.39
1995-96	46.16
1996-97	28.96
1997-98	25.00
1998-99	16.52
Total	270.27

Having regard to the pace of implementation, full Central assistance has already been released in respect of 14 growth centres. In as many as 23 growth centres, plots have been developed and allotment of plots has commenced. The other growth centres are at various stages of implementation. The budgetary provision for 1998-99 at revised estimate stage was Rs .25.23 crore.

Under the Prime Minister's new initiatives announced for the North-Eastern Region, a new Industrial Policy has been formulated for the North-Eastern Region which inter alla envisages that the entire expenditure on the growth centres in the North-Eastern

Region would be provided as Central assistance, subject to a ceiling of Rs. 15 crore per centre.

Transport subsidy scheme

The Transport Subsidy Scheme was introduced in July, 1971 to promote industries in hilly, remote and inaccessible areas. The Scheme is applicable to the States of Himachal Pradesh, Jammu & Kashmir, the North-Eastern States, Sikkim, Union Territories of Andaman & Nicobar Islands & Lakshadweep, Darjeeling District of West Bengal and eight hill districts of Uttar Pradesh comprising Almora, Chamoli, Dehradun, Nainital, Pauri Garhwal, Pithoragarh, Tehri Garhwal and Uttar Kashi. Under the Scheme, subsidy ranging from 50% to 90% is admissible on transport costs incurred on movement of raw materials and finished goods from designated rail heads/ports up to the location of the industrial units and vice-versa.

From the inception of the Scheme up to 3 1.03.1998, an amount of Rs. 360.77 crore has been released to the various States/UTs. In the Budget Estimates for 1998- 99, a provision of Rs. 85,00 crore has been made for the Transport Subsidy Scheme.

The Scheme is valid up to 31st March, 2000. However, the scheme has been extended up to 31st March, 2007 in respect of the North-Eastern Region.

Capital investment subsidy scheme

A new scheme, namely, Capital Investment Subsidy Scheme, 1997 has been introduced and notified on 1.6.98 under the Prime Minister's new initiatives for the North-Eastern Region. Under the Scheme, subsidy at the rate of 15% of the investment in plant and machinery, subject to a maximum ceiling of Rs. 30 lakh is payable to industries located in the Growth Centres and to new industrial units and/or their substantial expansion in other identified areas in the North-Eastern Region. The Scheme is operated through the State Government. The North-Eastern Development Financial Corporation (NEDFIC) has the Scheme has been extended up to 31st March, 2007 been designated as nodal agency to release subsidy in respect of the North-Eastern Region to the eligible units on the basis of recommendation of the State Level Committee/State Government.

7

Development of Promotional Organisations

Office of the economic adviser

Office of the Economic Adviser is an attached office to the Department of Industrial Policy and Promotion. The Economic Adviser is an Ex-officio member of the Bureau of Industrial Costs and Prices and Empowered Authority for National Renewal Fund. The main functions of the Office of the Economic Adviser include, inter-alia, the following :

— All aspects related to the formulation of Industrial and Trade Policies;

— Analysis of macro aggregates such as data relating to industrial production and trends in industrial growth as well as capacity utilisation, carrying out studies relating to various aspects of industrial development and growth, and preparing analytical reports, preparation of monthly reviews of industrial production, performance of infrastructure industries, performance of Public Sector Enterprises, release of advance information on industrial production, etc.

— Examination of general economic issues such as industrial finance, resource availability and mobilisation with reference to plan targets for the industrial sector, providing analytical back up and support to the nominees of the Ministry on the

Board of Term Lending Institutions and bringing out a monthly review on Current Economic Scenario and prospects;

— Analysis of fiscal proposals and duty levies;

— Compilation and publication of the official Wholesale Price Index Numbers in India every week, Periodical reviews of the trends in wholesale prices and bringing out of weekly, monthly and annual indices of wholesale prices;

— Monitoring of Annual Action Plan and preparation of performance reports;

— Coordinating the Research Work concerning Coordinating of work relating to monthly summary to Cabinet, comments on various Acts relating to Ceiling Laws, Industrial Relations, Companies Act, etc. and

— Compilation and publication of Hand Book of Industrial Policy and Statistics every year.

A Plan Scheme for conducting "Research Studies in Industrial Development" had been initiated in the Ministry of Industry in 1989-90. Under this, research projects are being undertaken within the Ministry of Industry as also in the research institutions on behalf of the Government of India.

The intention behind launching of these studies is to disseminate information on important issues with a view to encourage discussions and facilitate policy formulation. So for, under the series 21 study reports have been released. Seven of these studies are based on in-house research. All these studies have been well received and found to be extremely helpful in policy formulation as well as implementation of plan programmes for the industrial development of the country.

The Office has been supporting Market Information Survey of Households (MISH) survey by National Council for Applied Economic Research (NCAER) since 1986-87. The reports of earlier MISH survey have since been received from NCAER. These reports would be very useful in understanding the consumer expenditure on various consumer durables and non-durables. MISH is one of the most extensive surveys on consumer expenditure and the time series data should be extremely useful in planning capacities in these sectors.

Bureau of industrial costs & prices

Background

Bureau of Industrial Costs & Prices (BICP) was established in January, 1970 under the then Ministry of Industrial Development to advise the Government on a continuing basis on various aspects of the price structure, cost reduction and pricing in relation to industrial products. BICP started functioning with effect from April, 1970 as a focal and catalyst organisation, with an independent status.

Composition of the bureau &restructuring

The Bureau is a multi-disciplinary organisation and its work is organised in specialised divisions dealing with economic, costing and technical matters pertaining to industry. In addition to techno-economic and cost studies, the Bureau was before August, 1997, undertaking price studies for bulk drugs and recommending prices for the formulations of products covered under the Drug (Price Control) Order. Studies were also carried out with the objective of recommending appropriate levels of tariffs for different products and industries.

After the setup of "National Pharmaceutical Pricing Authority" (NPPA) in August, 1997, the work relating to bulk drugs and formulations alongwith the related manpower (33 officers) was transferred from BICP to NPPA.

In the context of economic liberalization, the Government of India also decided in Sept. 1997 to constitute an independent "Tariff Commission". Merger of the Bureau with the Tariff Commission is also under consideration of the Government.

The Bureau is headed by a full time Chairperson and Studies in Progress has a sanctioned strength of three full-time Members. The Economic Adviser to the Ministry of Industry Studies in International Competitiveness is an ex-officio Member of the Bureau and Adviser (Planning) to the Planning Commission is serving as a part time Member.

Functions of the bureau

BICP undertakes studies both suo-moto or on the basis of references made by Government Departments. The areas covered have been enlarged over the years to focus increasingly on infrastructural development and international competitiveness. BICP investigations cover the industrial sector as well as services, utilities and non-market organisations.

Since inception in 1970, BICP has, till Comprehensive Studies November, '98 submitted 858 Study Reports/Notes on various industries, service sectors and policy issues to the Ministries/Departments, Planning Commission and Cabinet Secretariat. Areas covered are:

— Price studies including those related to infrastructure;

— Tariff studies for streamlining/rationalising/harmonising the tariff structure-Customs & Excise;

— Resource efficiency studies;

— Studies in International Competitiveness; and

— Industrial Policy Issues including Industrial Monitoring and Development Studies

Studies completed

The submission of reports during the current financial year is as follows:

— Cost price study of Diammonium Phosphate (Indigenous and Imported) and Muriate of Potash (Imported);

— Price fixation of B-Twill Jute Bags;

— Establishment of Costing System and Estimation of Rates of Bank Notes for RBI;

— Report on the Indian Cellular Industry;

— Effective rate of protection of International Goods;

—Transfer price of Lakwa Gas Separation Plant of GAIL;

— Study on newsprint industry; and

— Fixation of service charges of metal handicrafts -MHSC, Moradabad.

Studies in progress

Studies in international competitiveness

Two studies which are in progress on international competitiveness relate to:-

— Comprehensive study of Steel Industry—this would cover both flat and non-flat products produced by primary and secondary steel products i.e. integrated steel plants and electric arc furnace route; and

— Ship Building Industry—assessing of prevailing shipbuilding costs and operational efficiency in the Indian shipyards and identifying measures for future growth and international competitiveness of the domestic shipbuilding industry.

Comprehensive studies

— Study covering the Aluminium industry including bauxite, downstream products and diversification; and

— Study on Coal focusing on the enhancement of competitiveness through cost reduction measures, technological upgradation, modernisation of production facilities, improvement in efficiency of resource-use along with environment and ecology

Price studies

— Rice milling charges for levy rice

— Cost studies for the following ten items under rate contract of DGS&D:-

— G.I. Pipes

— Hose pipes

— C.I. Spun Pipes

— A.C. Pressure Pipes

— Window Mounted type air-conditioner

— D.I. Spun Pipes

— Underground armoured cables

— Electrodes

— Fluorescent Tubes

— Energy Meters

Publications

The Bureau has been selectively publishing its reports, striking a balance between transparency in Government functioning and sensitivity of data. As a part of its continued efforts to share its information with scholars, experts and institutions interested in various areas of economic activity, the Bureau has published 32 reports so for. The reports published in the period under focus are:-

— Report on Sugar Industry;

— Report on Indian Telecom Cable Manufacturing industry.- and

— Hindi version of Report on Sugar Industry;

— In addition to the above, the Bureau is publishing reports on PSF and PFY during the current year.

Tariff commission

In keeping with the commitment to the economic reform process and to provide an independent regulatory body to look into tariff related issues, a Tariff Commission has been constituted in September, 1997.

The Commission is headed by a full-time Chairman of the rank of Secretary to the Government of India and will have a full-time member to be designated as Member- Secretary in the rank of Additional Secretary, apart from 3 to 5 other members.

With increasing openness in the Indian Economy, the terms of reference of the Commission have been revised, to provide it with requisite credibility and transparency. The revised terms of reference of the Tariff Commission are as follows:

— To make recommendations as an expert body, on matters referred to it by Government regarding fixation of tariff and all tariff related issues in relation to trade in goods and services, keeping in view the interest of various sectors including production, trade and consumers and taking into account the international commitments. The Commission should aim at evolving an overall tariff structure and look into the issue of tariff rationalisation;

— As per reference made by the Government, to study critically market access offers received from trading partners as part of WTO framework and to advise the Government on the opportunities and challenges generated by these offers;

— To make a detailed impact analysis on select sectors like textiles, agriculture, automobiles, information technology, chemicals, steel and engineering goods through a multi-disciplinary team;

— In order to facilitate the reforms process, the Commission may examine the transition-period required for select industries to recommend the gradual phasing-out of the tariffs as referred to it by the Government from time to time;

— To identify the tariffication process for select — economic activities as referred to the Commission by the Government from time to time;

— To monitor the tariff changes in the competing and trade-partner countries and maintain an inventory of tariff-rates at a sufficiently detailed level;

— To undertake such other tasks as may be assigned by the Government from time to time;

— To present an annual report to the Government of its activities;

— To carry out technical studies on cost of production of different goods and services and their competitiveness in relation to other countries; and

— To render advice on issues referred to it by the

Government on classification of goods, and products along with applicable tariff on such goods and products.

Office of the salt commissioner, Jaipur

The Salt Organisation with its Headquarters at Jaipur is headed by the Salt Commissioner who is assisted by 5 Deputy Salt Commissioners, 9 Assistant Salt Commissioners and other supporting staff. There are 5 Regional Offices functioning at Chennai, Mumbai, Admedabad, Jaipur and Calcutta besides the field offices in all the salt producing States.

The Salt Organisation is responsible for administration of Salt Cess Act, 1953 and the Rules made thereunder. The other main functions of the Organisation include planning of production targets, distribution of salt and price surveillance, promotion of technological development, maintenance of standards and improvement of quality of salt, promotion of exports, planning, formulation and monitoring of the execution of development and labour welfare schemes and custody and superintendence of Departmental salt lands.

The Salt Commissioner's office is identified as nodal agency for implementation of National Iodine Deficiency Disorders Control Programme (NIDDCP), a Plan Scheme being administered by the Ministry of Health & Family Welfare, in so for as it relates to production of iodised salt, monitoring of its quality at production level and its distribution to the consuming centres.

Office of the chief controller of accounts

The Departmentalised Accounting Organisation of the Ministry of Industry was set up in April, 1976 as a part of the Integrated Finance Wing, besides performing the payment & accounting functions for all the four Departments of the Ministry.

The Accounting Organisation is headed by a Chief Controller of Accounts who is assisted by one Controller of Accounts, One Deputy Controller of Accounts and 9 Pay and Accounts Offices in different parts of the country. The Principal Accounts Office in New Delhi functions as the administrative centre of the organisation. There is also an Internal Audit Wing with its headquarters at New Delhi.

8

Training, Research and Design Institutes

Central manufacturing technology institute, BangloreThe Central Manufacturing Technology Institute (CMTI), Bangalore, is an industry oriented R&D organisation in the area of manufacturing technology and provides technical assistance to machine tool and other engineering industries in the country in the design and development of machine tools, accessories, cutting tools and control systems, including CNC. In addition, the Institute provides technical information, training for engineers from industries and consultancy in manufacturing technologies, CNC/DNC/FMS, CAD/CAM/CAE/CIM, Robotics, Automation, Precision Engineering and Standardisation. Prototype testing is also undertaken.

CMTI is focussing its attention on development of modern machine tools, manufacturing technologies and systems to meet the current as well as future needs of Indian industries. Several high technology centres such as a NC Centre, a CAD/CAM Centre, a CIM Centre, a Precision Engineering Centre and a Robotic facility have been set up in the Institute.

The membership of the Institute is open to all engineering industries including the machine tool industry.

Under Eighth Five Year Plan, the following projects were completed:

— Computer Integrated Manufacturing (CIM) project with UNDP assistance to promote computer aided automation in manufacturing has been established;

— TQM Project to assist industries seeking ISO 9000 quality system certification with a team of well trained and qualified engineers has been created;

— A Precision Engineering Centre set up at the Institute is fully operational and is providing services to the engineering industry in the field of precision engineering. The Centre has facilities of an environmentally controlled precision machine shop and more closely controlled precision underground metrology laboratory. An on-going project of ultra Precision Engineering Centre with the objectives of design and evaluation of Ultra Precision Machine Tools and Measuring Equipment and development of Ultra Precision Manufacturing and Measurement technologies are envisaged; and

— Under Robotics facility project, the Institute undertakes design and development of manipulators/Robot Arms, Robot Controllers, Sensory applications, Automated Assembly Systems, ARC Welding and Deburring Cells. It also provides Robotic Arc Welding Services.

The following projects have been planned to be implemented during the ninth Plan Period:

— Modernization of Manufacturing facilities;

— Modernisation of Computer Systems;

— Modernization of Laboratories -

— Proactive Maintenance Engineering;

— Rapid Prototyping Centre,-

— Ultraprecision Engineering Centre; and

— Technology and Consultancy Centre for Small and Medium Engineering Industries.

The project planning and procurement of essential basic requirements for the prolects have been identified. Minimal facilities are being added in the areas of modernization of Manufacturing Facilities and Computer Systems.

Machining Technology Development tasks were carried out in several areas such as extrusion dies for ceramic catalytic converters, D Shaped slot in a component used in injection valve assembly etc.

Testing and Evaluation assignment completed during year include the Piston Ring Grooving and Turning Machine, CNC Keystone Piston Ring Grinder, Centreless Grinding Machine, Cam Turning Machine etc.

Software Packages such as Integrated Manufacturing Planning assembly schedule and control and manufacturing productivity analysis etc. were developed.

The National Information Centre for Machine Tools & Production Engineering (NICMAP) assisted by DSIR/ NISSAT, continued to provide information to industries, R&D units and Educational Institutions on products, processes, technologies, patents, etc. using Computerised databases developed by CMTI. Value Added Patent Information Service (VAPIS) Centre established in CMTI is providing consultancy and services to industries, R&D Units and Educational Institutions in the area of Patents.

14 Scheduled training programs, 2 Exclusive programs, 4 in-house programs, 3 special programs and one seminar were conducted involving 275 participants.

8 papers were presented in various Conference and Seminars. The Institute generated revenue to the extent of 80% of revenue expenditure during 1997-98 through its services to the industries.

Central pulp & paper research institute, Saharanpur

Background

Since inception(1980) the Central Pulp and Paper Research Institute(CPPRI) has been playing a significant role in improving the technical and technological competence of the Indian paper industry. Realising the need and necessity of R&D, CPPRI with the help of grants-in-aid from the Government of India has undertaken a series of R&D programmes for the non-wood based paper mills, which have helped in improving the technology and process paramete rs adopted by small mills.

The infrastructure and testing facilities of CPPRI have been strengthened through successive FAO, UNIDO and UNDP sponsored projects. As a result, it has developed high standard testing facilities for the pulp and paper industry. The institute is reorganising its activities to enhance its linkage with the industry. As a result, the internal generation of revenue of the Institute is increasing.

Activities and achievements during 1997-98

During the year 1997-98 the income of the Institute was Rs, 447.63 lakh, which include grant-in-aid of Rs. 380.08 lakh provided by the Ministry of Industry and Rs. 7.43 lakh received from Ministry of Non- conventional Energy Sources, as service charges and its internal generation as testing fee, consultancy fee, etc.

The Institute with its modern and well trained scientific and technical manpower, is taking a number of measures for improving its services. During the year 1997-98, the Institute undertook sponsored projects/ technical services from various paper mills and Government agencies like Bureau of Indian Standards, Directorate General of Supplies & Disposals, Directorate of Education, Directorate of Printing & Stationery, Ministry of Non-conventional Energy Sources, Energy Management Center, Central Pollution Control Board, etc. Sponsored projects include evaluation of raw material on laboratory and pilot plant scale, evaluation of paper making chemicals, analysis of fibrous and non-fibrous raw materials, analysis of spent liquor and calibration of various paper testing instruments.

The institute has also taken up research in the field of chemical recovery, air pollution and its impact on energy consumption and reduction in fresh water consumption in pulp and paper mills. The Institute concentrated on projects like clesilication of black liquor - transfer of technology, energy conservation in pulp & paper mills, development and utilisation of lignin by-products, setting up of Biotechnology Laboratory, elimination/reduction of chlorophenolic toxic materials, anaerobic/aerobic treatment of pulp & paper mill effluents, solid waste reduction and utilisation and status of air pollution in pulp & paper industry. Its Impact, Abatements and Management and Studies on manufacturing of highly filled papers. Apart from these projects the Institute continued to work on schemes such as Jute for international speciality pulp.

The Institute assisted the Ministry of Non-conventional Energy Sources in executing the UNDP/ GEF project of High rate biomethanation of pulp & paper mill wastes. A major project on utilisation of whole jute fibre, jute sticks and whole jute stalks for newsprint and paper making was sponsored jointly by UNDP and

Ministry of Textiles. The Institute also took up the project on Evaluation of Technologies for control of AOX in pulp & paper industry which was sponsored by Central Pollution Control Board. Revision of IS standard 5285-1969 was also undertaken by the Institute at the behest of Bureau of Indian Standards.

The Institute has made a breakthrough in Bio-energy recovery from agro-residue black liquor. CPPRI as a technology Institution has been assisting Ministry of Non-Conventional Energy Sources in execution of this project. Demonstration of High Rate Biomethanation plant was taken up at Satia Paper Mills in Punjab and was successfully commissioned and is running efficiently.

9

International Cooperation Including UNIDO

International cooperation division

In the wake of economic reform process initiated by the Government of India, the International Cooperation Division has been playing a catalytic role towards making Indian industry globally competitive.

International Cooperation Division continued to make efforts to increase cooperation with the developing as well as developed countries for mutual benefit through different institutions such as Joint Commissions/Joint Committees, other bilateral channels like interaction with the delegations visiting this Ministry etc., and organizing visits abroad for discussions on issues of mutual interest and attract foreign investment into India. This division participated in discussions covering International Cooperation organized by other Ministries and Departments of Government of India and also participated in the Joint Business Council Meetings organized by FICCI & ASSOCHAM jointly.

In view of the importance being attached to industrial cooperation and technological interface among Small and Medium Enterprises (SMEs) at the global level, Ministry of Industry has set up Country Specific Windows in respect of USA, Australia, France, Germany, Switzerland, Japan & South Korea. These countries have been identified considering the potentialities and mutual complementories for industrial and economic cooperation of higher levels.

Each Window is generating country specific data bank as well as information on Indian industry that is relevant to investors from these countries. They are providing necessary facilitation and coordination in selected cases and offer escort services. Nodal officers have been appointed to take up the responsibilities and coordinate activities relating to the specific Windows. The nodal officers also coordinate with State Governments and other agencies in order to solve any specific problem at the implementation level. Interactive meetings with the business communities of these countries have been held in association with FICCI as well as CH.

This Department acts the nodal Department for the following Joint Commissions:

— Indo-Swedish Joint Commission for Economic, Industrial, Technical and Scientific Cooperation;

— Indo-Libyan Joint Commission for Economic, Industrial Scientific and Technical Cooperation;

— Indo-Hungarian Joint Commission for Economic, Scientific and Technical Cooperation,- and

— Indo-Belarus Joint Commission for Economic, Industrial, Scientific and Technical Cooperation,

— Industry Minister is the Co-Chairman of these Joint Commissions.

Indo-EU Partenariat

One of the decisions taken at the last meeting of the India-EC Working Group on Trade and Economic Cooperation, was to consider holding an EU-India PARTENARIAT Business Meet in India. EU-India

PARTENARIAT, 1999, is a major Business Meet which will bring together up to 400 Indian and 400 European Union (EU) Small and Medium Sized Enterprises (SMEs) to discuss business partnerships, joint ventures, collaborations and strategic alliances. One-to-one prearranged business meetings will be organized with the help of a specially developed software. The venue is the Pragati Maidan, New Delhi, and the Meeting Days are 15th and 16th March, 1999.

Indo-belarus intergovernmental commission

1st Session of the Indo-Belarus Inter-Govern mental Commission on Economic, Trade, Industrial, Scientific, Technological and Cultural Cooperation was held in Minsk on October 26-27, 1998. The Indian delegation was led by the Hon'ble Industry Minister Shri Sikander Bakht.

During discussions in the Inter-Govern mental Commission the issues discussed covered bilateral relations; review of the current economic environment in India and Belarus, and review of cooperation in Industrial, Trade, Culture and Science & Technology sectors.

During his stay in Minsk, the Industry Minister called on the President and the Prime Minister of Belarus.

In order to have better industrial relations with Myanmar, hospitality was extended to a visiting four member delegation led by H.E. Mr. U. Thein Tun, Dy. Industry Minister - 2 of Myanmar by Hon'ble Minister of State (Industry) Shri S.S. Badal.

Steps have also been initiated for holding next meeting of the Indo-Hungary Joint Commission's meeting in Budapest and Indo-Libyan Joint Commission in Tripoli in the near future.

During the period under report, this Department

also actively participated in the meetings of various joint commissions/joint committees and other bilateral interactions like:-

- — Indo-Uganda Joint Commission Meeting;
- — Indo-Egyptian Joint Commission Meeting;
- — Indo-Iranian Joint Commission Meeting;
- — Indo-Japan Trade talks;
- — Indo-Croatian Joint Commission Meeting;
- — Indo-Austrian Joint Commission Meeting,-
- — Indo-EU Joint Commission Meeting;
- — Indo-Finish Joint Commission,-
- — Indo-Romania Inter-Session consultation;
- — Indo-EC Sub-Commission on (i) Trade and Commercial Cooperation, (ii) Economic Cooperation:
- — Indo-Bulgarian Joint Commission;
- — Indo-French Joint Committee;
- — Indo-Slovak Joint Committee; and
- — Indo-Czeck Joint Committee.

A large number of dignitaries from friendly countries and international agencies called on Hon'ble Industry Minister/Minister of State (Industry)/Secretary (IP&P) and held useful discussions on various aspects areas of industrial co-operation.

United nations industrial development organisation (UNIDO)

The United Nations Industrial Development Organisation (UNIDO) is mainly engaged in:

- — Strengthening of industrial capacities, which include promotion of investment and related technologies and programmes in support of global forum function and policy advice; and

— Cleaner and sustainable industrial development.

UNIDO provides specific assistance in comprehensive packages of integrated services in the following areas:

— Industrial Governance;

— Industrial Export Capacity building;

— Industrial Information Networking;

— International Industrial Partnerships;

— Quality and certification for industrial competitiveness;

— Cleaner industry and Environment;

— Efficient Energy Development;

— Agro-related Industrial Development,

— Local Industrial Development; and

— Women Entrepreneurship Development.

India, a founding member of UNIDO, is both a recipient and a contributor to the multifaceted industrial assistance and cooperation programmes. India makes a contribution to the tune of 0.43000/0' of the total budget of UNIDO and Voluntary Contribution equivalent to US $1 million which is mainly utilised for extending technical assistance from India to other developing countries.

Since, 1994 a series of Intechmarts have been organised which have been very well received by the Indian Industry and foreign investors. Presently, State level Intechmarts are being organised. Intechmart Gujarat '98 was held from 4-6 December, 1998 at Ahmedabad. It was organised by the Government of India, Ministry of Industry, Department of Industrial Policy and Promotion-

United Nations Industrial Development Organisation (UNIDO), the State Government of Gujarat and the Confederation of Indian Industries (CII). The event was well attended with significant foreign participation. A similar event is planned in West Bengal from 19-20 March, 1999 in Calcutta with the Joint collaboration of Government of India, UNIDO, CII and Government of West Bengal. This event would specifically focus on metal and engineering; Chemicals and petrochemicals including plastic; Electronics including software; Agro and food and Infrastructure.

In this Intechmart, participation is expected from countries such as Australia, Singapore, Japan, UK, Germany, Italy, France and Israel.

The Ministry of Industry is implementing UNIDO projects regarding capacity building for promotion of industrial investments in selected countries of Asia and Africa to enable them to explore their industrial development potentials. This objective is to be achieved through (1) strengthening of Entrepreneurship Development Institute of India, Ahemedabad, to assume the role of an inter-regional center for training in industrial project identification, preparation, appraisal and implementation as well as entrepreneurship development and (2) strengthening of national focal point institutions in participating developing countries. Other important projects which are under implementation include "Strengthening Technology Bureau for International Industrial Partnership" and "Regional Cleaner Production Centres."

During the year 1998, Department of Industrial Policy and Promotion have nominated 62 persons for training under the Colombo and bilateral training programmes. Under the UNIDO fellowship scheme, 31 foreign nationals were taken on conducted study tours in various technical institutions in India covering a wide range of specialisation.

India has been actively participating in the important meetings organised by UNIDO. The 19"' Session of Industrial Development Board and the 14th Session of Programme and Budget Committee were attended by senior officers. India also participated in a Special High level Round Table meeting on Industrial Development in the 21st century which was held in UNIDO from 4-6 May, 1998. The 20st Session of the Industrial Development Board was held from 19-20 November, 1998 in Vienna.

10

Automotive Industry

A sound transportation system plays a pivotal role in the country's rapid economic and industrial development. The well-developed Indian automotive industry ably fulfils this catalytic role by producing a of wide variety of vehicles: passenger cars, light, medium and heavy commercial vehicles, multi-utility vehicles such as jeeps, scooters, motorcycles, mopeds, three wheelers, tractors etc. The automotive industry comprising of the automobile and the auto component sectors has shown great advances since delicensing and opening up of the sector to FDI in 1993.

The investment in the industry is Rs. 29,868 crore up to 1997-98. The turnover of the automobile industry exceeded Rs. 36,500 crore in 1997-98. Including turnover of the auto-component sector, the automotive industry's turnover exceeded Rs. 47,000 crore. The contribution of this industry to the exchequer stands at Rs. 31714 crore during 1997-98. The industry provides direct employment to 4.5 lakhs and generates indirect employment of one crore. The contribution of the automotive industry to GDP has risen from 2.77% in 1992-93 to 4.40% in 1997-98.

Since liberalisation in 1993-94 to 1996-97, the automobile sector has shown a spectacular overall growth rate of over 20% in the number of vehicles manufactured. Also this period was characterised by the entry of global automobile manufacturers for setting up joint ventures in

India. The investment envisaged in these projects are to the tune of US $ 3.6 billion. There has been substantial addition to capacity creation from 1993-94 to 1997-98, installed capacity in 4 wheelers had increased from 5.2 lakh to 12.96 lakh vehicles.

The exercise of capacity building is on-going, though with a shift in the market segment. While 1996 and 1997 where characterised by accretion to the medium segment car production, in 1998 the capacity creation is for the smaller compact cars which are coming into the market during the year i.e. Hyundai, Daewoo and TELCO cars, to vie with Maruti for this sizeable market. Two model of small cars viz. Santro by Hyundai and Matiz by Daewoo motors have already been introduced. Telco have also released their small car in December, 1998. Some of the joint ventures commenced production in 1996-97 and the industry was faced with intense competition particularly in the mid-segment of passenger cars.

The intense competition is a positive feature showing the health of the Industry. However, this has come in a period when the Indian economy and industry have slowed down. It resulted in the industry having to bear the brunt of demand constraint, which set in 1996-97. The sustained demand constraints through 1997-98 however has had a telling effect on the industry. 1997-98 witnessed a drastic decline of 33% in production of medium and heavy commercial vehicles. Nevertheless, thanks to surge in two wheeler productions in 1997-98, overall automobile sector maintained production levels, logging a marginal rate of growth of 0.5%.

While the automotive industry had made spectacular strides with average growth rate 20% from 1993-94 to 1996-97, owing to slow down of the economy; this industry has been passing through, a phase of sluggish growth during the years 1997-98 and 1998-99. Of late, passenger car industry is also facing fall in demand. The estimated percentage of growth in production during 1998-99 over 1997-98 is shown below. It is expected that the Automotive sector will have a positive growth rate from the year 1999-2000 onwards.

S.I. No.	Item	Estimated growth in production during 1998-99 over 1997-98.
1.	Commercial vehicles	-33%
2.	Cars	+2%
3.	Multi-utility vehicles	-17%
4.	Two wheelers	+7%
5.	Three wheelers	-17%

The Swiss major Volvo has commissioned their new unit near Bangalore introducing trailer type trucks from June 1998. It has been interpreted that the present overall decline in industrial growth was essentially a difficult phase that Indian industry was passing though owing partly to 'cyclical' factors that can be expected to correct themselves. Further, the slack industrial performance was mainly due to dampened investment activity arising from high level of uncertainly and excess capacity build-up in some sectors, including automobiles.

To overcome the general slow down in the economy, the plan outlays on key infrastructure sectors have been enhanced to 35% in the Union budget 1998-99. Specially, the allocation of Rs. 500 crore for new road projects would benefit the revival of commercial vehicle segment in the lost quarters of 1998-99. Further, number of other specific measures to boost up the demand, particularly for the CV segment, suggested by the working group is likely to be announced (any time now) in the ensuing budget proposals.

Automobile components

Government have already brought out comprehensive automobile policy which encourage not only additional foreign direct investment in to the country but also higher level of indigenisation at a reasonable pace.

The growth of automobile components industry is closely linked to the growth of automotive industry, as substantial quantity produced is supplied by auto components industry to original equipment manufacturers. Keeping in line with the growth in production/ sales of automobile over the past few years, auto components industry has also registered slow growth. The production during 1997-98 was of the order of Rs. 12000 crore compared to Rs. 11500 crore during 1996-97 registering growth of 5%.

However, no growth is expected during 1998-99 due to fall in production of commercial vehicles and passenger cars. Major automobile manufacturers have set up ancillary groups with technical collaboration/ subsidiary arrangements with renowned manufacturers of auto components abroad. In fact some of the foreign manufacturers are in the process of setting up Indian production base to cater to the global demand for auto components like DELPHI, TACS, HYUNDAI Joint Ventures, HONDA Joint venture.

The automobile industry is also contributing to the export efforts of the country. Export has been growing consistently over the years, though there has been some setback due to global recession and South-East Asian crisis. The details of export in 1996-97 and 1997-98 are given below. On export front, automobile component sector has registered a growth rate of 19% during 1997-98. Total export of auto component during 1997-98 was of the order of Rs. 1239 crore compared to Rs. 1070 crore during 1996-97.

(Quantity in Nos.)

S. No.	Export	1996-97	97-98	Growth (%)
1.	Medium/Heavy commercial vehicle	6606	4554	-31%
2.	Light commercial vehicle	7230	8023	11%
3.	Cars	37161	29747	11%
4.	Jeeps	2484	3261	31%
5.	Two-wheelers	114724	125504	9%
6.	Three-wheelers	21973	18595	-15%
7.	Auto components	Rs. 1033 crore	Rs. 1239 crore	19%

According to a study, automobile exhaust contributes more than 60% of the atmosphere pollution in metropolitan cities. With the growing number of vehicles, the pollution in the cities is ever increasing. Pollution control strategy of Government relies upon notifying emission standards to encourage industry to develop new and better technologies to prevent pollution at source. Government has, accordingly, notified stricter emission norms both for petrol driven and diesel vehicles effective from April 1996 under the Motor Vehicles Act.

The Indian automobile manufacturers have already met these norms. With the availability of unleaded petrol in the metropolitan cities from 1995, fitment of catalytic converters on new petrol driven four wheelers in the Metros has been made compulsory.

The exercise for fixation of even stricter norms by 2000 for various types of automotive vehicles has already been completed and notified by the Ministry of Surface Transport. These emission norms are one of the most stringent in the world. Manufacturers are adopting various routes to achieve 2000 norms and are confident of becoming successful.

Agricultural machinery

Agricultural Machinery mainly contains Agricultural Tractors, Power Tillers, Combine Harvesters and other machinery and implements.

Agricultural tractors

At present, there are ten units in the organised sector manufacturing agricultural tractors covering a wide range from lower Horse Power in the range of 16-20 HP to higher Horse Power of 50 HP and above. The Industry made a beginning in 1961 with a total production of 880 units. There has been a substantial growth in the production of tractors since late 1980s and the production has reached a level of 256258 numbers in 1997-98 having a growth rate of 16%. Production figures of tractors during the last few years are given below:-

Year	Numbers
1994-95	1,62,900
1995-96	1,91,149
1996-97	2,21,743
1997-98	2,56,258

Though tractor industry started production by importing technology from renowned manufacturers in USA, UK, USSR, Germany, Poland, Czechoslovakia etc. over the years, technology has been fully absorbed. Some tractor manufacturers have introduced higher Horse Power tractors of 75 HP with imported components for meeting the specific requirements of high HP category of tractors.

The production of tractors in the range of 3 1-40 HP is around 60%, in the range of 41 HP and above is 23%

and below 30 HP category is 17% of the total production. Traditionally, Haryana, Punjab and Uttar Pradesh are the main States for the tractor market. The new markets for tractors in the States of Madhya Pradesh, Andhra Pradesh, Tamil Nadu, Maharashtra and Gujarat States are growing at a faster pace. Government has been laying special emphasis on promotion of small HP tractors. Exemption from excise duty has, therefore, been granted to tractors with an engine capacity of up to 1800 cc.

Diesel engines

The Diesel Engine industry provides prime movers of vehicles and equipments, which are portable and mobile. These engines also find application in agriculture machinery, generating sets, fishing boats, ocean gain vessels, earthmoving machinery, locomotives etc. The engines manufactured in the country cover a wide range from 5 HP to 10,000 HP.

The present trend of diesel engines for all earth-moving machinery has been on in line/'V' type naturally aspirated/turbo charged six cylinders/four cylinders water cooled engines. Apart from this, fuel efficient and low emission turbo charged engines for vehicular applications are also being made indigenously. However, engines using non-conventional sources are being thought of. Production figures of diesel engines for the last few years are given below :

Year	Production in numbers
1995-96	1,82,443
1996-97	2,36,460
1997-98	2,67,630

Power tillers

Power Tiller is a hand operated tractor specially designed

for use by small and medium size farmers and under-farming conditions where large tractors are not suitable and uneconomical to operate. Manufacture of power tiller in the country was introduced in 1960s with technology imported mainly from Japan. Only two manufacturers of power tillers are presently operating in the organised sector. Power Tillers are manufactured in the range between 8-13 HP. Power Tillers are used in cultivation of rice, sugarcane, horticulture, orchards, low crop cultivation crop production and bound farming. Production figures of power tillers are indicated below :-

Year	Production in numbers
1995-96	9950
1996-97	11210
1997-98	13018

Self propelled combine harvesters

With growing emphasis on farm mechanisation Self-propelled Combined Harvesters have been introduced in the Indian agricultural scene during late 1970s. These Harvesters have gained popularity among the farmers, particularly in North India. Presently there are two units in the organised sector manufacturing these Harvesters which are more suitable for harvesting paddy crops. These two units have produced 339 Nos. in 1996-97 and 195 Nos. in 1997-98

Earth moving and construction machinery

Earth Moving Equipment and Construction Machinery Industry play a vital role in the economic development of our country. This industry is closely linked with major development and infrastructural schemes such as coal and mineral mining, irrigation and power projects, ports, steel, fertilizers etc. The technology required to manufacture such machines was not earlier available. It was, therefore, necessary to permit import of technology for development of the same from internationally reputed manufacturers like KOMATSU, CATERPILLAR, POCLAIN, DRESSER of UK, DEMAG AND HITACHI.

The earth moving equipment currently being manufactured cover Shovels up to 10 cu.m. capacity, Bulldozers up to 770 HP, Dumpers up to 120 HP, Excavators up to 8.5 cu.m. capacity. Scrapper and Motor Craders up to 280 HP and walking Draglines, Mobile cranes etc.

Construction equipment, mainly road construction equipment such as graders, loaders, excavators vibratory compactors, hot mix plants etc. are being manufactured indigenously.

These machines help to speed up development in irrigation and power projects, coal and iron ore mining, for excavation of lime stone for cement, for development and reclamation of fast track of land, building roads, making canals, preparing industrial sites and all facets of the country's development activity. These machines also reduce dependence on labour and provide automation in construction work.

Indigenous production of Earth-moving and Construction Machinery commenced in 1960s. Today, there are 32 units engaged in the manufacture of various types and sizes of Earth-moving and Construction Machinery and country is, by and large, self-sufficient in respect of these items. In fact, during the last decade, the industry has made enormous progress and has grown both in size and diversity. Presently, there are over 40,000 units of Earth Moving and Construction Machinery operating in the Country.

The total capacity available in the Earth Moving & Construction Equipment Industry is around 6000 nos.

With the Government's emphasis and priority on the development of infrastructure, this group of industry is expected to grow in near future.

The number of Earth-Moving and Construction Equipment manufactured during last 4 years is given below:-

Year	Production in numbers
1994-95	2216
1995-96	3769
1996-97	4734
1997-98	5182

11

Industrial Sectors

As a result of sound policies pursued over the years, tremendous development has taken place in India industry, which stands today on a sound footing. However, there are certain infrastructural weaknesses which need to be tackled to ensure further growth. Indian indústry has undergone a sea change since Independence. From a situation, where even a pin had to be inported, India has reached a stage when it is going to manufacture 50-seater and 100-seater passenger aircraft. What is more, the Indian consumer today has a wide variety of goods to choose from. The Indian market place is today. loaded with a range of goods. Whether it is newer models of cars, scooters or mlobikes, washing machines, sooking range or mixies there ia large variety to choose from. Gone are the days when choices were limited and one had to wait almost a year to get delivery of a new car or a scooter. One can today walk into a show room and drive out. With a choice available to the consumer the quality of goods have also shown distinct improvement.

Indian industry at the time of Independence was at a rudimentary stage. It was confined to cotton and jute textiles, which accounted for 56.8 per cent of value-added in manufacturing sugar (6.6 per cent), engineering (8.4 per cent), steel (7.6 per cent), chemicals (4.1 per cent) and cement (2.1 per cent). Modern industry formed only six to eight per cent of national income in Independence India in 1950, with small scale enterprises and mining contributing 12 to 14 per cent. A feature of India's industrial sector soon after Independence was the virtual absence of capital or producers goods industry. Indian industries had to rely almost wholly on imported machinery and machine tools. In 1950, India met 89.8 per cent of its need for machine tools through imports, producing internally only Rs. 30 lakh worth of machine tools and portable tools.

The foundations of modern India's industrial economy was laid by Jawaharlal Nehru, who led the country to freedom and thereafter as Prime Minister for nearly 17 years, built the country's economy form a scratch. This was done through the public sector, whose foundations were laid by Nehru, as the private sector did not have the resources to undertake huge infrastructure projects, like Bhakra hydro-electric power project, or steel plants like Bhilai, whom the great visionary described as the temples of modern India. Nehru realised that without the basic infrastructure industries, the foundations of a modern industrial economy could not be laid. If this war true in 1950, it is equally true today as infrastructural bottlenecks are constraining growth.

Industrial growth after Independence was facilitated by the Industrial Policy Resolution of 1948, followed by the Industrial Policy Resolution of 1956, which had as its objective, the acceleration of the rate of economic growth and the speeding up of industrialisation as a means of achieving a socialist pattern of Society. In 1956 capital was scarce and the base of entrepreneurship was not strong enough. Hence the 1956 Industrial Policy Resolution, gave primacy to the role of the state to assume predominant and direct responsibility for industrial development. Special importance was given in the two resolutions of 1948 and 1956 to the development of steel, heavy engineering, machine tools and heavy chemicals industry.

The industrial policy resolution of 1948 has a small number of industries to be reserved for production by the public sector. These included the production and control of atomic energy and ownership and managment of railways. However, coal, iron and steel, aircraft manufacturing, shipbuilding, manufacture of telegraph and wireless equipment (except radios) and minerals were reserved for production by Central or State government undertakings. The 1956 industrial Policy Resolution added some more industries to the list. The original thinking was that as far as the public sector was concerned, it should enter fields where private sector would find it difficult to invest. By 1956, this had changed to an absolute preference for state ownership of industries and the public sector was supposed to capture the commanding heights of the economy.

Since Independence, the public sector in India has been guided by the Industrial Policy Resolution of 1956, which had as its objectives the acceleration of the rate of economic growth and speeding up of the industrialisation as means of achieving the socialistic pattern of society. Since in the initial phase of industrialisation, the capital was scare, the state sector assumed the predominance and direct responsibility for industrial development. The size of public sector in India is indeed very large. It includes government departments and its compaines whether in the Central or state sector, irrigation and power projects, railways, posts and telegraphs, ordnance factories and other departmental undertakings, banking, insurance, financial and other services. The focus here is however, on the Central public sector enterprises established as Government companies or statutory corporations excluding banking units.

After the initial exuberance of public sector entering into new areas of industrial manufacturing, providing technical services, trading, financial and services sectors, the public enterprises started facing various problems, some of these problems were due to historical reasons, while others were related to poor project management, over-manning, obsolete technology, poor order book positions etc. All these put together, the public sector as a whole started showing results far below the desired level in comparison to the investments made in them.

The Government announced a new Industrial Policy on 24 July 1991 which envisages liberalisation, competitive environment. The new Policy has laid down certain specific areas in respect of the public enterprises which are to be emphasized in order to make them better performers and more competitive. The slient features of the new Industrial Policy on the Public Sector are: (i) Portfolio of public sector investments will be reviewed with a veiw to focus the public sector on strategic, high-tech and essential infrastructure. Whereas some reservation for the public sector is being retained, there would be no bar for area exclusively to be opened up to the private sector selectively. Similarly, the public sector will also be allowed entry in areas not reserved for it; (ii) Public enterprises which are chronically sick and which are unlikely to be turned around will for the formulation of revival, rehabilitation schemes, be referred to the Board for Industrial and Financial Reconstruction (BIFR), or other similar high level institutions created for the purpose. A social security mechanism will be created to protect the interest of workers likely to be affected by such rehabilitation packages; (iii) in order to raise resources and encourage wider public participation, a part of the governement's share-holding in the public sector would be offered to mutual funds, financial institutions, general public and workers; (iv) Boards of public sector companies would be made more professional and given greater powers; (v) there will be a greater thrust on performance improvement through the Memoranda of Understanding (MOU) system through which management would be granted greater autonomy and will be held accountable. Technical expertise on the part of the Goernment would be upgraded to make the MOU negotiations and implementation more effective; and (vi) to facilitate a fuller discussion on performance, the MOU singed between Government and the public enterprise would be placed in Parliament. While focussing on major management issues, this would also help place matters on day to day operations of public enterprises in their perspective.

As a major step for implementation of the Policy, the Government of India has disinvested varying percentage of its share-holdings in some PSUs. So far, the shares of 39 PSUs, have been disinvested in favour of the financial institutions, mutual funds, banks, foreign institutional investors and the public. This resulted in disinvestment of 152.07 crore share in 39 public sector undertakings and a sum of Rs. 9,794 crore was realised.

The shares of these companies are now listed on the stock exchanges. The valuation of the equity of these enterprises on the stock exchanges reflects the preceptions of the public in general and investors in particular of the performance and the expectations of the public from these enterprises. Besides, the Government has also offered a part of its equity holdings in some of these enterprises in favour of the employees, in order to encourage the employees participation in the managements a sence of commitment and belonging to an enterprise.

Over a period of time, the public enterprises have been faced with the chronical sickness and mounting losses. In the case of some of the enterprises, which have incurred huge losses and had eroded their networth, in order to formulate the revival/rehabilitation packages, a number of these enterprises have been referred to the Board for Industrial and Financial Reconstruction (BIFR). So far, 54 sick enterprises have been referred to BIFR for revival/rehabilitation. BIFR makes an independent assessment of the viability or otherwise of a particular enterprise afte keeping in the view points of the owner (Government), the employees, the financial institutions and the other concerned. Under the new Industrial Policy, greater thrust has been laid on the evaluation of the performance, through the system of MOUs which has also started yielding positive results in the form of better performance from the public enterprises.

There has been appreciable growth in the investments in the public sector over the years. In 1951, the investment in five Central Public Sector was Rs. 29 crore. This investment has gone up to Rs. 147,587 crore in 245 enterprises as on 31 March 1993 and at Rs. 164,332 crore in 246 enterprises in 1993-94. Thus, during 1993-94, the investment in public sector has increased by Rs. 16,745 crore registering an increase of 11.35 per cent.

Public sector has been playing a dominant role in the fertilizer industry. The first state-owned fertilizer unit was set up in 1951 at Sindri in Bihar, which was followed by another plant at Nangal in Punjab. With the coming up of another fertilizer plant at Trombay, Government decided to bring all the public sector fertilizer units under the management of a single undertaking and the Fertilizer Corporation of India Limited (FCI) was accordingly incorporated in January 1961. The National Fertilizers Limited was established on 23 August 1974.

Thereafter, the Fertilizer Corporation of India and the National Fertilizers Limited were re-organised into four companies on the basis of feedstock used and geographical considerations from 1 April 1978. At present, there are nine public sector undertakings under the administrative control of Department of Fertilizers. FCI has now four units, one each at Sindri (Bihar), Gorakhpur (U.P.) Talcher (Orissa) and Ramagundam (Andhra Pradesh), with a total installed capacity of 5.87 lakh tonnes of nitrogen.

The National Fertilizers Limited (NFL) has, at present, five operating units, *viz.*, the calcium ammonium nitrate plant at Nanagal and the urea plants at Nanagal, Bhatinda, Panipat and Vijaipur. With the commissioning of the Vijaipur plant in 1987-88, the total installed capacity of NFL has gone up to 10.36 lakh MT of nitrogen, making NFL the largest producer of nitrogenous fertilizers in the country.

The Fertilizers and Chemicals Travancore Limited (FACT), Udyogamandal (Kerala), has, at present, three operating units, one at Udyogamandal and two at Cochin. Besides fertilizers, the company is engaged in the manufacture of chemicals. With the commissioning of caprolactum plant in October 1990, the company has entered the field of petro-chemicals also. FACT Engineering and Design Organisation (FEDO), another division of the company is engaged in design, engineering, procurement, supervision of construction and commissioning of fertilizers/chemical plants.

Rashtriya Chemicals and Fertilizers Limited (RCF) is in charge of the Trombay plants and the large gas-based fertilizer plant at Thal which started commercial production in 1985. Hindustan Fertilizer Corporation Limited has five units in production, three at Namrup in Assam and one each at Durgapur in West Bengal and

Barauni in Bihar, having total annual installed capacity of 6.54 lakh tonnes of nitrogen. Madras Fertilizers Limited (MFL) is a joint venture, with the Government of India holding 67.55 per cent of the equity share capital and the National Iranian Oil Company holding the remaining 32.45 per cent.

The annual installed capacity of MFL is 1.76 lakh tonnes of nitrogen and 1.12 lakh tonnes of phosphate. Pyrites, Phosphates and Chemicals Limited (PPCL), set up in March 1960, is presently engaged in the exploration of pyrites deposits as well as production of single super phosphate at Amjhore in Bihar, exploration-cumproduction mining of pyrites deposits at Saladipura in Rajasthan and mining of rock phosphate ore from the Mussuoorie phosphorite deposits.

Projects and Development India Limited (PDIL), formerly known as Fertilizer (Planning & Development) India Limited, is engaged in design, engineering, procurement and supervision of construction/ commissioning of fertilizer and allied chemical plants. The company has played a pioneering role in developing, entirely on its own initiative, the know-how for manufacture of catalysts in India. Pradeep Phosphates L:imited (PPL) was established in December, 1981 for setting up a phosphatic fertilizer complex at Paradeep in Orissa. Phase-I of the project, comprising 7.20 lakh TAP capacity DAP plant and allied facilities was commissioned in 1986. Phase-II of the project, comprising sulphuric acid and phosphoric acid plants, also went into commercial production in June 1992.

Indian Farmers Fertilizer Cooperative Limited (IFFCO) incrporated in 1975 and Krishak Bharati Cooperative Limited (KRIBHCO) incorporated in 1985, are the two cooperative sector undertakings under the administrative control of the Department of Fertilizers.

IFFCO has four operating units, one each at Kalol and Kandla in Gujarat and Phulpur and Aonla in Uttar Pradesh. KRIBHCO has a gas-based urea-ammonia plant at Hazira in Gujarat with a capacity to produce 14.50 lakh tonnes of urea per annum. The combined installed capacity of IFFCO and KRIBHCO is 15.31 lakh tonnes of nitrogen and 3.09 lakh tonnes of phosphate.

The assumption on the savings front is that the public sector would be able to return positive savings to the tune of 2.8 per cent of GDP. Currently, the net dissavings in the government sector in in the order of one and-a-half per cent, while the public secor undertakings return positive savings, amounting to a little over three and-a-half per cent GDP.

However, the scope for the latter to increase further is limited, as the share of public sector units' (PSUs) output in the GDP gradually declines in the wake of reforms that seek to confer a larger role to private capital. In fact, it would not be surprising if the PSU savings as percentage of GDP actually came down. With public sector saving at 2.8 per cent of GDP, the government (both at the Centre and the States) needs to bring down their dissavings substantially. It implies a substantial curb on profligacy sundrome, further fiscal consolidation and an impressive step-up in tax revenues.

The Ninth Plan of Rs. 27.2 lakh crore at 1996-97 base prices would have about 40 per cent of the resources allocated for the public sector. This would include Rs. 3.76 lakh crore as budgetary support. But then, growth is not just a question of gross investment—its sectoral distribution as also the policies that direct it are equally relevant. And, it is here that the government holds the key entirely. In fact, any particular level of budgetary support to the Plan makes little sense without refernce to its sectoral allocation. Budget funds are required to meet the investment needs of sectors that will not attract private funds, particularly the social sectors. The government must, therefore, first prioritze the sectors and then discuss the amount it would invest during the Plan period.

While raising resources would be the major problem during the Ninth Plan period, the Centre and the States wouls have to increase tax rates, remove the loopholes in tax laws and improve collection. There is need for steps by the Centre and the States to increase tax-GDP ratio for additional resource mobilization. The suggestion made by the West Bengal Chief Minister, Mr. Jyoti Basu, for tapping black money sources to raise resources and to ensure that people having black money are forced to part with a slice of their ill-gotten wealth for developmental purposes is worth considering.

Among the various policies enunciated for restructuring of the PSUs, a major step involved the disinvestment of a part of Government equities in selected public undertakings for improving their performance as well as to increase their public accountability by broad basing their management and ownership. In the process of disinvestment, a major step taken by the government has been to set up the Disinvestment Commission for working out the terms and conditions as well as modalities pertaining to disinvestment of public equities. At present the government contemplates restructuring of equity in 40 major PSUs, including blue-chip companies like ONGC, GAIL, SAIL, MTNL, IPCL, NTPC, BEML, Power Grid, NHPC, IOC, IBP and Bongalgoan Refineries. While the Commission is to determine the modalities of disinvestment, the actual sale of PSU shares would be done through Deptt. of Public Enterprises (DPE). The Commission also intends to identify the non-core PSUs where the Government may even disinvest by more than 50 per cent and may have minority ownership.

Under auspices of the National Renewal Fund (NRF) set up in February 1992, for mobilising funds to assist voluntary retired persons from PSUs in undergoing re-training and re-deployment, Rs. 252 crore and Rs. 217 crore were released in 1994-95 and 1995-96, respectively. An estimated number of 87,800 workers have opted for voluntary retirement so far and a major portion of NRF has been utilised in the textile sector.

Indistrial relations have shown a steady improvement in the years follow the economic reforms. Mandays lost due to strikes and lockouts declined significantly from 22.97 million in 1992-93 to 17.99 million in 1995-96. This was mainly due to improvement in the industrial relations situation in cotton, engineering, coal and non-coal mining, beverages, tobacco & tobacco products, jute and rubber industries. During 1992-96, industrial unrest was witnessed mainly in the states of Andhra Pradesh, Gujarat, Tamil Nadu and Maharashtra, Government's proactive role through timely and effective conciliation of industrial disputes and involvement of the social partners in the formulation and implementation of labour and industrial relations policies and programmes has successfully harmonised the interests of employers and workers.

First company legislation in India was an Act for registration of joint stock companies enacted in 1850. This was followed by the Companies Act, 1913. As a result of recommendations of a committee under the chairmanship of C.H. Bhabha to make suggestions for company law reform, the Companies Act, 1956 was enacted as a Central lefislation. Prior to enactment of this Act, administration of companies' legislation was the responsibility of the state governments.

The Companies Act, 1956 has been in force for the last 38 years and during this period it has been amended over 16 times. Amendments of 1969, 1974, 1977 and 1988 are of special importance. By the amendment Act of 1969, system of appointing managing agencies or secretaries or treasurers in companies was abolished. Under the 1974 amendment, powers of High Court relating to certain sections of the Companies Act were transferred to Company Law Board. Scope of Section 43A was enlarged so as to treat large private limited companies as deemed public limited companies. A new Section 58A was inserted to regulate acceptance of deposits by companies. Section 108A to Section 108H were introduced to check take-over bids by large groups.

The 1977 amendment inserted, inter alia Section 634A enabling Company Law Board to enforce its orders under Section 17, 18, 19, 79 141 and 186 of the Act as a decree of a court of law. The Companies Act, 1956 provides various powers to Central Government and Company Law Board, to monitor, regulate and control the affairs of companies.

Salient features of the 1988 amendments are: (a) setting up of an independent Company Law Board to exercise such judicial and quasi-judicial functions as are presently being exercised either by Court or Central government and proposed to be transferred to that Board; (b) dispensing with Government approval for managerial appointments and remuneration, subject to fulfilment of certain statutory guidelines which are proposed to be incorporated in the Act itself; (c) delinking of rates of depreciation from rates specified under the Income Tax Act and laying down rates of depreciation in the Act itself to reflect true and fair view of the state of affairs of the company; (d) protecting the interest of investors by providing for intervention by Company Law Board against non-payment of public deposits and certain other matters, compulsory redemption of preference shares in certain cases, requiring companies to disclose reasons for refusal to register transfer of shares, protecting the rights of thee transfere pending mutation of his name in the register of members, and also compulsory lilsting of all public issues; (e) reducing unnecessary cost or burden by requiring companies to attach only an abridged version * for disclosure of information relating to conservation of energy, technology absorption, foreign exchange earnings and outgo as well as particulars of employees having some minimum stake in the company and drawing remuneration in excess of that drawn by managerial personnel.

The number of joint stock companies, both Government and non-Government incorporated under the Companies Act, 1956 and at work in India as on 31 March 1994 was 3,08,324. Of these 3,05,625 were limited by shares, 349 with unlimited liability and 2,350 were limited by guarantee or were associations not for profit. The 3,05,625 companies limited by shares have paid up capital of Rs. 1,04,890.8 crore. These comprised 38,000 public limited companies and 2,67,625 private limited companies with paid up capital of Rs. 70,112.1 and Rs. 34,778.7 crore respectively.

The primary objective of the Government's policy for Small and Tiny Enterprises would be to impart more vitality and growth impetus to the sector to enable it to contribute its mite fully to the economy particularly in terms of out put, employment and exports. In this context, it is heartening to note that at the end of the 7th Plan period the small scale sector accounted for mearly 35 per cent of the gross value of the out put in the manufacturing sector and over 40 per cent of the total exports from the country.

It also provided employment opportunties to around 12 million people. To ensure the growth of the Small and Tiny sector the Government proposes to review and modify all Statutes, regulations and procedures wherever necessary, to ensure that their operations do not militate against the interest of small and village enterprises.

As mentioned earlier in this paper, manufacturing units with an investment and plant and machinery up to * 75 lakhs and units which are willing to undertake an export obligation to the extent of 30 per cent of their annual production by 3rd year with an investment of Rs. up to 75 lakhs are eligigle for small scale registration. The investment limit in respect of Tiny Enterprises has been increased from Rs. 2 lakhs to Rs. 5 lakhs. With the objective of providing support to the service sector in view of its potential for generating employment, it has been decided that in future all industry related service and business enterprises irrespective of their location would be recognised as small scale industries and their investment ceiling would correspond to those of Tiny Enterprises.

Units in the small scale sector (other than Tiny Enterprises) would be entitled to benefits like preference in land allocation, power connection, access to facilities for skill/technology upradation. Tiny enterprises would in addition to these benefits will also be eligble for additional support including easier access to institutional finance, priority in the Government purchase programme and relaxation from certain provisions of labour laws.

Inadequate access to credit-both short—term and long—term remains a perennial problem facing the small scale sector. Emphasis would henceforth shift from subsidiese/cheap credit, except for specified target groups, and efforts would be made to ensure both adequate flow of credit on a normative basis, and the quality of its delivery, for viable operations of this sector. A special monitoring agency would be set up to oversee that the genuine credit needs of the small scale sector are fully met. To provide access to the capital market and to encourage modernisation and technlogical upgradation, it has been decided to allow equity participation by other industrial undertakings in the SSI, not exceeding 24 per cent of the total shareholding. this would also provide a powerful boost to ancillarisation and subcontracting, leading to expansion of employment opportunities.

Regulatory provisions relating to the management of private limited companies are being liberalised. A Limited Partnership Act will be introduced to enhance the supply of risk capital to the small scale sector. Such an Act would limit the financial liability of the new and non-active partners/entrepreneurs to the capital invested.

A beginning has been made towards solving the problems of delayed payments to small industries by setting up of factoring services through Small Industries Development Bank of India (SIDBI). Network of such services would be set up throughout the country and operated through commercial banks. A suitable legislation will be introduced to ensure prompt payment of small industries' bills.

To facilitate location of industries in rural/backward areas and to promote stringer linkages between agriculture and industry, a new Scheme of Integrated Infrastructural Develpoment (including Technological Back-up Services) for Small Scale Industries would be implemented with the active participation of State Government and Financial Institutions. A beginning in this direction will be made this year itself.

A Technology Development Cell (TDC) would be set up in the Small Industries Development Organisation

(SIDO) which would provide technology inputs to improve productivity and competitiveness of the products of the small scale sector. The TDC would coordinate the activities of the Tool Rooms, Process-cum-Product Development Centres (PPDCs), existing as well as to be established under SIDO, and would also interact with the other industrial research and development organisations to achieve its objectives.

Adequacy and equitable distribution of indigenous and imported raw material would be ensured to the small scale sector, particularly the tiny sub-sector. Policies would be so designed that they do not militate against entry of new units. Based on the capacity needs, Tiny/Small Scale Units would be given priority in allocation of indigenous raw materials.

A proper and adequate arrangement for delivery of total package of incentives and services at the District level will be evolved and implemented.

Inspite of the vast domestic market, marketing remains a problem area for Small and Tiny Enterprises. Mass consumption labour intensive products are predominantly being marketed by the organised sector. The Tiny/Small Scale Sector will be enabled to access existing support mechanism. Market promotion would be undertaken through cooperative/public sector institutions, other specialised/professional marketing agencies and consortia approach, backed up by such incentives as considered necessary.

National Small Industries Corporation (NSIC) would concentrate on marketing of mass consumption items under common brand name and organic links between NSCI and State Small Industries Development Corporations (SSIDCs) would be established.

Government recognises the need to widen and

deepen complementarity in production programmes of large/medium and small industrial sectors. Parts, components, sub assemblies, etc. required by large public/private sector undertakings would be encouraged for production in a techno-economically viable manner through small scale ancillary units. Industry associations would be encouraged to establish subcontracting exchanges, in addition to strengthening the existing ones under the SIDO. Emphasis would also be laid on promotion of a viable and competitive component market.

Though the small scale sector is making significant contribution to total exports both direct and indirect, a large potential remains untapped. SIDO has been recognised as the nodal agency to support the small scale industries in export promotion. An Export Development Centre would be set up in SIDO to serve the small scale industries through its network of field offices to further augment export activities of this sector.

A greater degree of awareness to produce goods and services conforming to national and international standards would be created among the small scale sector.

Industry Associations would be encouraged and supported to establish quality counselling and common testing facilities. Technology Informaton Centres to provide updated knowledge on technology and markets would be established.

Where non-conformity with quality and standards involves risk to human life and public health, compulsory quality control would be enforced.

Are-oriented programme of modernisation and technological upgradation aimed at improving productivity, efficiency and cost effectiveness in the small scale sector would be pursued. Specific industries in large concentrations/clusters would be identified for studies in conjunction with SIDBI and other banks. Such studies will establish commercial viability of modernisation prescriptions, and financial support would be provided for modernisation of these industries on a priority basis.

Indian Institutes of Technology (IITs) and selected Regional/other Engineering Colleges will serve as Technological Information, design and Development Centres in their respective command areas.

Government will continue to support first generation entrepreneurs thrugh training and other measures. Large number of EDP trainers and motivators will be trained to significantly expand the Entrepreneurship Development Programmes (EDP). Industry Associations would also be encouraged to participate in this venture effectively.

EDP would be built into the curricula of vocational and other degree level courses. Women entrepreneurs will receive support through special training programmes. Definition of "Women Enterprises" would be simplified. The present stipulation regarding employment of majority of women workers would be dispensed with and units in which women entrepreneurs have majority shareholding and management control, would be defined as "Women Enterprises"

Additional employment opportunities would be generated through training of multi-disciplinary barefoot managers to suit special requirements of the small scale sector.

The persistent complaint of small scale units of being subjected to a large number of Acts and Laws, being required to maintain a number of registers and submit returns, and face an army of inspectors, would be attended to within a specified time frame of three months.

Procedures would be simplified, bureaucratic controls effectively reduced, unnecessary interference eliminated an paper work cut down to the minimumto enable the entrepreneur to concentrate on production and marketing function.

The Government has also announced a number of steps for promoting Handloom sector, handicrafts sector and other village industries.

A number of organisations are engaged in exploration and development of mineral resources in India. These include Geolgical survey of India (GSI), Indian Bureau of Mines (IBM) and a number of public sector undertakings under the administrative control of the Ministry of Mines.

Geological Survey of India functions as the premier national organisation for earth science, entrusted with the task of scientific survey and research for locating mineral resources (except oil, natural gas and atomic minerals), systematic generation and continous updating of geoscience information through ground, airborne and marine survey, the entire gamut of activities being related to multifarious developmental needs of the country. The survey operates within the ambit of its charter 1873 and priorities laid down by the Government.

The other important functions of the organisation cover management of natural hazards like earthquake, floods, landslides, volcanism etc., providing geotechnical advice to all the major civil engineering, communication and urban development projects, geoenvironmental resource appraisal, upgradation of geoscientific expertise through training. The results of GSI investigations are documented in the form of scientific and technical reports, professional papers, maps, inventories and various types of publications.

The survey with its central headquarters at Calcutta, functions through six geographically based regions, three activity based Wings (Marine, Coal and Airborne Survey) and one training Institute. In each of the region/wings towards * greater collaboration and setting up of consultancy and commercial endeavours in the third world countries.

The Indian Bureau of Mines (IBM) is the national organisation under Ministry of Mines and engaged in promotion, conservation and scientific development of mineral resources of the country other than coal, petroleum and natural gas, atomic minerals and minor minerals. It performs regulatory functions, namely enforcement of Mines and Minerals (Regulation & Development Rules and the provision of Environmental Protection Act.

It also undertakes scientific techno-economic, research-orientid studies in various aspects such as geological, mining ore beneficiation and environment. IBM provides technical consultancy services to the mining industry for geological appraisal of mineral resources and preparation of feasibility reports of mining projects including beneficiation plants. It prepares mineral maps and countrywide inventory of minerals resources of leasehold and freehold areas.

IBM also functions as data bank for mines and minerals and publishes statistical periodicals and brings out technical publications/monogrphs on individual mineral commodities and bulletins on different connected subjects. it advises the Central and state governments on all aspects of mineral industry, trade and legislation. It imparts training to technical and non-technical officials of IBM and also persons from mineral industry and other agencies in India and abroad. IBM is organised into six functional agencies in India and abroad. IBM is organised into six functional divisions. It has its headquarters at Nagpur and 11 regional offices and well equipped ore-dressing laboratories and Pilot Plant at Nagpur, besides, two regional ore-dressing laboratories at Ajmer and Bangalore. IBM also has a big Central Library with about 61,000 books.

Public sector

Minral Exploration Corporation Limited (MECL) was created in 1972 with the main objective of bridging the gap between the disc overy of mineral prospect and its eventual exploitation. Its identified major functions are to plan, promote, organise and implement programme for the exploration of mineral resources and to perform such functions as Central Government may from time to time, assign to the company in connection with exploration of the mineral resources in and outside the country.

The Corporation has its headquarters at Nagpur. MECL has fulfilled its main objective by establishing over 55,000 million tonnes of reserves of higher confidence for veriety of minerals. The drilling capacity of 72,000 m per annum at the time of inception in 1972 has increased to 4.25 lakh metre of drilling and mining capacity has increased from 1200 mtr in 1972 to 9000 m in the last year of Seventh Five Year Plan. During 1993-94, the turnover of the company was Rs. 40.73 crore.

Bharat Aluminium Company Limited (BALCO) was incorporated on 27 November 1965 as the first primary aluminium producing undertaking in the public sector. The Company is operating Korba Aluminium Complex in Bilaspur district of Madhya Pradesh and Bidhanbag Unit in Asanosl in west Bengal. It has a capacity to produce one lakh tonnes of aluminium metal/products. During the past few years, the Company's production of saleable metal/products has been about 92,000 tonnes per annum.

Its net profit has been going up steadily and during 1994-95, it earned a net profit of Rs. 90.51 crore (provisional). The new projects of the Company include installation of a new Cold Rolling Mill having an installed capacity to produce 40,000 TPA of thin quality sheets/coils. The Comapny is also in the process of modernisation of their smelter plant at Korba for increased productivity and reduction of power consumption, which is a major factor in input costs.

National Aluminium Company Limited (NALCO) was incorporated on 7 January 1981 with the objective to produce alumina and aluminium. Its registerd office is at Bhubaneswar. It operates a bauxite mine to raise 24 lakh tonnes per annum of bauxite from the Parnchpatnali (Koraput) deposits, an eight lakh tonnes per annum alumina refinery at Damanjodi (Koraput), a 2,18,000 tonnes per annum aluminium smelter at Angul (Dhenkanal) and six 120 MW captive power plants at Angul to feed the smelter. Aluminium Pechiney of France was the technical consultants for the project and had supplied the technical know-how and basic engineering package.

NALCO received ISO 9002 Certification from IROS for Alumina Refinery on 21 November 1994 and ISO 9002 Certification for quality system for Smelter Plan in March 1995 from RWTUV. Highest production of calcined alumina of 81,000 MT during January 1995 exceeding the rated capacity. NALCO produced 1,78,072 tonnes of aluminium and earned net profit of Rs. 294.62 (provisional) during the same period.

Hindustan inc Limited (HZL) was incorporated on 10 January 1966 to take over operations of the earstwhile Metal Corporation of India Limited and to develop mining and smelting capacities to substantially meet the domestic demand of zinc and lead metals. With headquarters at Udaipur, HZL's operations are spread over in the states of Rajasthan, Andhra Pradesh, Orissa and Bihar consisting of five mines with a total lead-zinc ore production capacity of 3.04 million tpa and four smelters with combined installed capacity of 1,49,000 tpa zinc and 65,000 tpa lead besides a rock phosphate and tungsten mine. The company offers a wide range of zinc and lead metal grades to its customers, besides a range of by-products.

The production of zinc metal by the company during the last four years has ranged between 84,600 tpa and 1,19,810 tpa. The lead production during the same period has ranged between 30,300 tpa and 34,500 tpa. The sales turnover of the company during 1994-95 was Rs. 97,274 lakh and its net profit (after tax) during the same period was Rs. 7,643 lakh.

HZL signed a Memorandum of Understanding with M/s. Niugini Mining Limited.Australia, to identify gold resources in India and later on if resources are found viable, to set up a joint venture. It has also signed an MoU with M/s. BHP Minerals, Austrails, for exploration and development of base and procious metals in Rajasthan. Besides, HZL and BRGM, France, have reached an agreement with Vietnam Rare and Precious Metal Corporation (VMC) for setting up of joint venture for exploration and development of Pac Lang Gold Prospect in Vietnam.

Hindustan Copper Limited (HCL) is the sole producer of primary copper metal in the country. It was incorporated on 7 November 1967, to take over from the National Mineral Development Corporation, projects, schemes and studies pertaining to exploration, exploitation, mining and smelting of copper. In 1972, the erstwhile Indian Copper Corporation Limit, a company incorporated in England was nationalised and merged with HCl. The main projects of the company are: (i) Khetri Copper Complex (KCC) in Rajasthan comprising Khetri, Kolihan, Chandmari and Dariba mines (since closed), concentrators at Dariba (since closed) and Khetri, Metallurgical and fertilizer plants at Khetri; (ii) Indian Copper Complex (ICC) at Ghatsila in Bihar comprising Mosaboni, Fathargora, Kendadih and Rakha Mines, three concentrators at Mosaboni, Moubhandar (since closed) and Rakha and metallurgical plants for copper and by-product recovery at Moubhandari (iii) Malanjkhand Copper Project (MCP) at Malanjkhand in Madhya Pradesh comprising an open pit mine, concentrator and leach copper plant; and (iv) Taloja Copper Project (TCP) at Taloja in Maharashtra for conversion of cathodes both imported and part of our own into continuous cast copper wirerods as value added product.

The company produces primary copper products in the form of cathodes, wirebars, wirerods and is also engaged in manufacturing of single super phosphate, sulphuric acid, gold, silver, selenium, tellurium, palladium, copper sulphate and nickel sulphate as by-products.

The current operation plants of the company are to produce and market about 70,000 Mt copper in different forms out of which 45,000 MT of refined copper is produced from indigenous ore resources. With the changed economic scenario in the country, HCL has initiated process of restructuring of companies to remain competitive. During 1994-95, the turnover of the company was Rs. 932.95 and its production of refined copper was 46,134 MT.

Bharat Gold Mines Limited operates the world famous century old Kolar Gold Mines in Karnataka State. The company was nationalised in 1956 and was incorporated as a public sector company under the

Department of Mines, Government of India in March 1972. Though the gold mining is the principal activity of the company, as a corporate stategy, it has diversified into the field of mine construction and contract works, manufacture of mining machinery and components of equipment.

The company has three major activities namely: (i) Gold mining: Two mines in Kolar Gold Fields, Karntaka-Mysore Champion Amalgamated mine and Nundydroog mine, and three mines in Andhra Pradesh, Yeppamana mine, (Anantapur); Chigargunta mine; and Old Bisanatham mine, (Chittoor); (ii) Mine Project and Construction Division-Taking up mine construction and development works for other mining (coal and metal mines) industries all over India, and (iii) Workshop Diversification-The workshops manufacture mining machineries and components of certain equipment and undertake jobbing works, like machining and fabrication for major industries in the country.

The company's registered office is at Koar Gold Fields and its liaison office is at New Delhi. In 1994-95, the company produced 650.28 kg of gold.

The continued financial losses over the decade has resulted in the company being declared as a sick industry and consequently referred to Board for Industrial and Financial Reconstruction (BIFR) who have appointed ICICI as Operating Agency to formulate a rehabilitation package envisaging increase in gold production from the existing shallow mines to ensure economic viability, exploration and exploitation of gold from the BGML lease-hold areas in collaboration with a suitable joint venture partner and to recover gold from old mill tailings accumulated over the years by constructing a suitable gold recovery plant by BGML.

Sikkim Mining Corporation was established as joint venture of Sikkim State and Government of India in 1960 by proclamation of erstwhile "Sikkim Darbar". the objective of the Corporation is to mine multimental ore for production of copper, lead and zinc concentrates. The Corporation has only one mine (Bhotang Mine) Situated at Rangpo (East Sikkim). During 1994-95, the Corporation produced 270 mt tonnes of copper concentrate, 85 mt of lead concentrate and 568 mt of zinc concentrate. Zinc concentrate is being sold to M/s. Hindustan Zinc Ltd. since April 1994. Hindustan Copper Limited has stopped taking copper concentrate, M/s. HAMCO Mining and Smelting Limited, Calcutta, has lifted 3,500 tonnes of lead, 200 tonnes of copper and 200 tonnes of zono concentrates on trial basis in the year 1994-95.

The National Mineral Policy, 1993, announced on 5 March 1993, in brief, had dispensed with the reservation of all the minerals reserved for exclusive exploitation by public sector and also for the first time, sought to invite foreign investment in the mining sector. The amendments to the Mines and Minerals (Regulation & Development) Act, 1957 seek to further elaborate the principles enunciated in the National Mineral Policy by, among others, devolving more powers to the state governments, providing greater stability of tenure in mining leases and by accelerating inflow of private capital, both domestic and foreign, as also the state-of-the-art technology into the mineral sector.

The amended Act has deleted 15 minerals hitherto listed in the First Schedule of the MM (R&D) Act, 1957 requiring prior approval of the Central Government before the state government could grant a prospecting licence of a mining lease. The minerals so deleted are apatite and phosphatic ores, barytes, dolomite, gypsum, kyanite, magnesite, molybdenum, nickel, platimum and other precious metals, sillimanite, silver, sulphur and its ores, tin, tungsten and vanadium ore. With this deletion (excepting the atomic minerals and fuel minerals), there would only be 11 minerals left for which the state government would require prior approval of the Central Government. These are asbestos, bauxite, chrome ore, copper ore, gold, iron ore, lead, limestone (except where it is used in kilns for the manufacute of lime as building materials) manganese ore, precious stones and zinc. the amended Act has removed any restriction on equity holding by foreign nationals in a mining company.

As of now, any company registered or incorporated in India can apply for a prospecting licence of a mining lease from the concerned state government. For the first time, a minimum period of lease of 20 years, has been made mandatory. The maximum period for grant of lease has been increased to 30 years.

Further renewals are possible with approval of the Central Government. The period for which prospecting licence can be granted has been increased to three years and these licences can be renewed at the discretion of the state governments so that the total period does not exceed five years. The amended Act also provides that no appeal or revision will lie to the Central Government against orders passed by the state governments with regard to minor minerals. State governments have also been empowered to terminate leases of minor minerals without prior approval of the Central Government. The amended Act also introduces a new section, whch gives powers to carry out searches to check unauthorised mining.

The Act, was amended to increase the period before which a lease can lapse from one year to two years. In addition, the amendment also provides that notifications issued by state governments under their minor minerals concession rules must be placed before the State Legislature and also empowers the Central Government to modify leases not in conformity with the Act to bring them in line with the provisions of the MMR&D Act, 1957.

The history of modern iron and steel industry in India began in 1870 when the Bengal Iron Works Company set up its plants at Kulti in West Bengal. However, the first effort at large scale production got underway when the Tata Iron Steel Company (TISCO) was set up at Jamshedpur in 1907. This was followed by the establishment of Indian Iron and Steel Company (IISCO) at Burnpur in 1919.

The first unit in public sector now known as Visvesvaraya Iron and Steel Limited (VISL) started functioning at Bhadravati in 1923. After Independence, though development of steel industry was considered during the First Plan, it was only during the Second Plan period that efforts were made to set up three integrated steel plants each with 10 lakh ingot tonnes capacity at Bhilai, Durgapur and Rourkela. An expansion programme to double the capacity of the two private sector steel plants, namely, TISCO and IISCO to 20 lakh tonnes ad 10 lakh tonnes respectively was also taken up.

The three plants in the public sector came into existance in stages between 1956 and 1959 and the expansion of the private sector plants was completed in 1959. During the Third Five Year Plan, emphasis was laid on the expansion of the three public sector plants and preparation of plans to set up three more steel plants at Salem (Tamil Nadu). Vijaynagar (Karnataka) and Visakhapatnam (Andhra Pradesh) to create additional steel production capacity in the Fifth Plan.

Steel Authority of India Limited (SAIL) is a wholly-owned government undertaking. It is responsible for the management of steel plants at Bhilai, Durgapur and Rourkela, Bokaro and Burnpur and also the Alloy Steel Plant at Durgapur an the Salem Steel Plant. The management of IISCO was taken over the Government on 14 July 1976 with a view to improving its working. The company is now a wholly-owned subsidiary of SAIL. SAIL took over Maharashtra Elektrosmelt Limited, a mini steel plant producing ferro-manaanese and steel in January 1986. Visvesvaraya Iron and Steel Limited, a unit controlled by the Karnataka Government was taken over by SAIL in August 1989.

Authorised capital of SAIL and paid up capital, as on 31 March 1995 are Rs. 5,000 crore and Rs. 3,985.89 crore respectively. The turnover during 1994-95 was Rs. 13,688.54 crore (excluding IISCO). Production of crude steel, saleable steel and pig iron from steel plants under SAIL (excluding IISCO) during 1993-94 and 1994-95.

Apart from the integrated steel plants, steel is also produced by electric arc furnace units which are popularly known as mini steel plants, from steel scrap/ sponge iron. While integrated steel plants mainly produce mild steel in bulk quantities, the mini steel plants produce mild seel as well as alloy steels including stainless steels. From this sector, crude steel production during 1994-95 was 2.9 million tonnes (provisional).

The New Industrial Policy announced in July 1991 has removed iron and steel from the list of industries reserved for the public sector, and also exmpted it from the requirements of compulsory licensing. Enterpreneurs are, therefore, free to set up steel plants of any capacity, subject to certain locational restrictions.

Iron and steel has also been placed in the list of high priority industries where, subject to certain conditions, automatic approvals are available for foreign equity upto 51 per cent, and for technology agreements upto specified limits. There has been a very positive response from the entrepreneurs. A capacity of about 7.5 million tonnes for producing various categories of steel involving an investment of about Rs. 13,142 crore is in various stages of implementation.

Rashtriya Ispat Nigam Limited was incorporated as a public sector company in February 1982 to implement construction of the first shorebased Integrated Steel Plant in th country located at Visakhapatnam, Andhra Pradesh. The project has been completed in two stages: first stage was completed by March 1992 and the second and final stage by July 1992.

Visakhapatnam Steel Plant (VSP) is the most sophisticated modern integrated steel plant in the country. Some of the most modern technologies adopted in the plant are: seven metre tall coke ovens, dry quenching of coke with auxiliary power generation facilities, 3200 CuM blas furnaces, conveyor charging and bell-less top charging for blast furnaces, cent per cent continuous casting of liquid steel and sophisticated high speed rolling mills. VSP's manpower, considering its size is lowest in the Indian steel industry. Though the production in Visakhapatnam Steel Plant commenced in the year 1991-92, 1993-94 was the first full year of integrated operation.

Visakhapatnam Steel Plant has achieved high levels of techno-economic and operating performances during 1994-95 creating records in the Indian steel industry and surpassing the DPR Norms. On the marketing front, VSP ended the year with a turnover of about Rs. 2,266 crore, which is 19 per cent higher than that of the previous year. Domestic sales of steel showed substantial increase with sales volume registering 1.2 million tonnes, a 43 per cent growth over 1993-94. Exports accounted for 4.65 lakh tonnes of iron and steel with a total realisation of Rs. 471

crore in foreign exchange. By-product sales registered a turnover of Rs. 147 crore which is 65 per cent higher than what was achieved in the previous year. VSP made a cash profit of Rs. 55 crore (provisional), for the first time, as against a cash los of Rs. 233 crore made in 1993-94.

At present, rubber goods industry comprises of 32 tyre units, 220 medium scale units, 5,500 small scale units and an equal number of units in the tiny sector. It offers direct and indirect employment to over seven lakh people. There is an investment of about Rs. 3,500 crore and a turnover of over Rs. 7,000 crore in this industry. The major rubber goods produced by the industry are tyres and tubes of all kinds, surgical gloves, prophylactics, conveyor and vee belts, instruments, hose pipes, sport goods etc. Tyres and tubes constitute the most important segment of this industry. Of the total investment, over Rs. 2,000 crore have been in the tyre and tubes industry. This industry has been identified as of extreme focus for export purposes.

The export of tyres and tubes which was Rs. 593 crore in 1993-94 is expected to reach Rs. 750 crore in 1994-95 and Rs. 1,000 crore by 1995-96. The exports of rubber goods other than tyres and tubes are also steadily growing.

Over the years, engineering industries in the country have registered a phenomenal growth to generate a strong base in a wide-range of heavy and light engineering industries covering a broad spectrum of capital goods and consumer durable products. Bulk of capital goods required for power projects, fertilizer plants, cement plants, steel plants, mining equipment and petro-chemical plants are being met from indigenous production. Construction machinery and equipment for irrigation project, diesel engines, pumps and tractors for agriculture, vehicles, etc., transport are also being met from within the country. Engineering industries have also demonstrated their capacity to manufacture large size plants and equipment for virous sectors such as power generation, fertilizers and cement.

Machine Tool industry is the backbone of entire engineering sector. This industry which till few years back was confined to the manufacture of conventional machine holding has now geared itself to meet the growing challenge of a diverse requirement from the user sector.

Heavy electrical industry comprises equipment used for the generation, transmission, distribution and utilisation of power. It includes items such as generators, boilers, tubines, transformers, switchgears etc. The indigenous industry is equipped to meet the entire domestic requirement. The established capacity in the country for manufacture of thermal and hydro-power generating equipment is around 4,500 mw and 1,345 mw respectively. Most of these capacities are in the public sector, in companies such as BHEL. The entire industry has been delicensed under the New Indusrial Policy announced by the Government of India. Also under the new Policy, these items qualify for automatic approval as regard to foreign collaborations.

Stream and hydro turbines are manufactured both in the public and private sector. The total capacity is over 7,000 mw. The public sector undertaking BHEL has the largest capacity. Steam turbines upto 500 mw unit rating are being manufactured by BHEL. It also manufactures gas turbines.

Boliers of both the categories, namely, for industrial and power applications are being produced in the country. For power boilers, BHEL is capable of making boilers for super thermal power plants. M/s. ABL Durgapur, is a major unit manufacturing power boilers.

There are 19 manufactures of industrial boilers in the country. The production of fludised bed boilers using biomass, agricultural waste, inferior grades of coal etc., has also started both for process application as well as for generating power.

There are 33 units in the organised sector manufacturing power and distribution transformers. The technology and design of power transformers manufactured in the country are comparable with the international standards. Manufacturing facilities for dry type distribution transformers have been established in th country. The technology and manufacturing facilities for amorphous core transformers and aluminium foil wound transformers are being established.

In the context of power system development in evolving a National Grid by end of current Plan period, conceted efforts are on for strengthening the transmission system by execution of 400 KV lines, introducing HVDC back-to-back tie lines, phased conversion of AC lines into DC lines and implementing load despatch and communication links besides system improvement measures by installing adequate reactive compensation system and PF correction capacitor banks.

AC transmission in 800 KV class has been adopted as the standard for the next higher level. Indigenous industry is technology sufficient in transmission system upto 400 KV reactive compensation system upto 220 KV and is in the process of indigenisation of HVDC technology and development of 800 KV class equipments. A total switchover to all Alluminium Alloy Conductors (AAAC), realising its techno-economic benefits, would give a boost to this sector.

The electrical industry covers a wide range of products which includes white goods (refrigerators, washing machines, air-conditiones, etc.), house-hold, electrical appliances, electrical, fans, storage batteries, dry cells, power cables, telecommunication cables, electrical motors and electric lamps. The installed capacity is considered adequate to meet the domestic demand as well as exports. Under the new industrial policy, the entire industry has been delicensed. Many of the electrical items like electric motors, jelly filled cables, optic fibre cables and pumping sets also qualify for 51 per cent foreign equity and automatic foreign collaboration under the new industrial policy.

In the field of telecommunication, capacity has also been created for manufacture of optical fibre cables. Hindustan Cables Limited, a Government of India undertaking, and the Madhya Pradesh State Electronic Development Corporation, an undertaking of the Government of Madhya Pradesh, have been permitted to establish capacities for the manufacture of OFC to the extent of 40,000 and 20,000 fibre km per annum respectively.

Keeping in view the safety and quality aspects of household electric appliances, Government have introduced compulsory ISI marking in respect of electrical immersion heaters, electrical iron, electrical stove and plugs and sockets.

Various steps have been initiated to ensure adequate testing facilities and availability of quality raw materials and components to the manufactures in order to help them conform to the requirements of the said scheme. There has been a greater consumer awareness about the quality and safetyof these goods.

The need for energy conservation has ensured greater focus in the manufacture of energy efficient electrical lamps. The industry is receiving adequate encouragement from the Government. A number of foreign collaborations have already been apporoved for manufacture of energy efficial lamps.

In the storage battery industry, some new units are coming up. The process of upgradation of technology in this industry is continuously benefiting the customers. The industry has started providing batteries to Maruti Premier 113 NE and Contessa Classic apart from light commercial vehicles.

The crane industry has a good potential for growth in the coming year in view of increased port and container handling activities and other projects like steel plant modernisation. Considerable investment is this area has been made by the indigenous crane manufactures. By and large the indigenous manufactures are capable of meeting the demand. The industry is delicensed.

At present there are eight units in the country engaged in the manufacture of lifts and escalators. The present installed capacity of these units is of the order of 3000 Nos per annum. A new range of lifts known as Sky Climbers has been/is under manufacture indigenously. These lifts are used for maintenance of TPS boilers/ bridges etc., and are being produced for the first time.

As elsewhere in the world, there is an increasing shift in India to have large power houses particularly Super Thermal Power Stations. Consequently, while there would be fewer but larger power generating stations, the demand for transmission line towers for transmission of energy would grow substantially. There are at present 25 manufacturing units reporting production to Ministry of Industry. There is sufficient capacity available in the country for manufacture of different types of transmission line towers. The industry is delicensed subject to locational angle.

Paper is a vital and core industry for any country

and per capita paper consumption can be taken as a measure of growth and progress in areas related to industrial, cultural and educational activities. Per capita consumption in India is less than three kg as against more than 300 kg in highly developed countries.

The origin of the paper industry could be traced back to 1812 when first paper mill was set up at Serampur, West Bengal. At present there are more than 350 mills in the country with an annual installed capacity of around 37 lakh tonnes. A significant aspect of the paper industry is strong presence of smaller paper mills with an installed capacity of 33,000 tonnes per annum or less. They account for nearly 50 per cent of the total installed capacity and contribute about 50 per cent to the production of paper and paper board in the country.

Capacity utilisation of the paper industry has declined from 96.35 per cent in 1952 to about 60 per cent in 1994. Various reliefs and concessions have been extended in recent years to help the industry to improve its capacity utilisation and financial viability. These include liberalisation facility for import of raw materials, low excise on use of minimum 75 per cent non-conventional raw materials *viz.* bagasse, jute, wheat/rice straw, waste paper, etc., delicensing the manufacture of certain varieties of paper etc.

At present, the country is self-sufficient in respect of common varieties of writing and printing paper and paper board and only certain special varieties of papers are being imported. The import of paper has been brought under OGL and customs duty on import of paper has been reduced from 65 to 20 per cent in this year. The demand of paper and paper board up to the end of the Eighth Plan is likely to be met by some new mills, revival of the some of the closed mills, modernisation and expansion of some of the existing units. In order to encourage use ofnon-conventional raw material, paper units based on use of minimum 75 per cent pulp derived from bagasse, agricultural residues and other non-conventional raw materials have been exempted from industrial licensing subject to locational policy.

Until 1981, National Newsprint and Paper Mills recently known as *nepa* Limited which commenced in 1955 was the only unit in the country manufacturing newsprint. As on 1 January 1995, there are 22 newsprint mills in the country with an annual installed capacity of 5.50 lakh tonnes. However, one newsprint mills *viz.* rayalseema Paper Mills Ltd having an annual installed capacity of 20,000 TPA is lying closed.

Demand for newsprint is met by indigenous production supplemented by imports. Import of newsprint which was decanalised earlier, has been decontrolled with effect from 1 May 1995. Now, import of newsprint is under OGL. The customs duty on the import of newsprint has been abolished with effect from 25 July 1991 in respect of standard newsprint and with effect from 1 march 1992 in respect of glazed newsprint. The production of newsprint for 1994-95 was about 4.02 lakh tonnes.

Cement, an important infrastructure core industry, is one of the most advanced industries in the country. Till about a decade ago, the country was deficient in cement and it had to resort to import in order to fill the gap in supply. After the complete de-control of price and distribution on 1 March 1989 and introduction of other policy reforms, the cement industry has made rapid strides both in capacity/production and in production and process technology. At present there are 107 large plants with an installed capacity of about 79 million tonnes. In addition, there are about 250-300 mini cement plants with an estimated capacity of seven million tonnes. The total operative installed capacity is estimated to be around 86 million tonnes. In 1993-94, production of cement was 57.96 million tonnes against a target of 60 million tonnes. The Production target fixed for 1994-95 was 62 million tonnes. With a production of 62.35 million tonnes, the industry was able to achieve the target. The growth rate recorded during the year was 7.6 per cent. During the year the capacity utilitisation has also increased from 80 per cent in 1993-94 to 86 per cent.

India is producing different varieties of cement the ordinary portland cement (OPC), portland pozzolana cement (PPC), portland blaster furnace slag cement (PBFS), oil well cement, white cement, etc. These different varieties of cement are produced strictly under BIS specifications and the quality is comparable to the best of the world.

Apart from meeting the entire domestic demand for cement, the industry is also exporting a large quantity. The export of clinker and cement has increased from 0.36 million tonnes in 1990-91 to 1.18 million tonnes in 1992-93 and 2.85 million tonnes in 1993-94. The export in 1994-95 was to the tune of 3.38 million tonnes.

Utilising a part of the funds provided by the World Bank to the cement industry and the grant from DANIDA, Denmark, a Human Resource Development Project is being implemented for providing demand driven training to the operators, line managers and supervisors to enhance their skills for handling latest equipments.

Four regional training centres have been set up and equipped with various classroom equipments, special equipments, computers, books, manuals and other training aids at ACC, Jamul (M.P.), Dalmia Cement,

Dalmiapuram (T.N.), J.K. Cement, Nimbahera (Rajasthan) anmd Gujarat Ambuja, Ambuja Nagar (Gujarat). A large number of personnel of the cement industry and part-time trainers have already been trained in these RTCS. Fourteen training packages have already been developed abroad and 18 more are presently being developed.

Another innovative pilot project for bulk transportation and distribution of cement is being implemented with World Bank assistance at Kalamboli, New Bombay. Department of Industrial Policy and Promotion and the Associated Cement Companies Ltd. (ACC) are participating directly in the project. Under this project, special high.

The drugs and pharmaceuticals industry in India, during the last 40 years has shown tremendous progress if one takes into consideration the growth rate as seen in other developing countries. Today, India is in a position to meet 70 per cent of its requirement of bulk drugs and almost all its requirement of formulations. The industry continued to maintain the steady growth in terms of production as well as range of products in 1993-94 alslo. During 1994-95, the production of bulk drugs and formulations is estimated to be of the order of Rs. 1,518 crore and Rs. 7,935 crore respectively, showing a growth rate of 15 per cent over the previous year's production. In the case of individual drugs, where decrease in production has taken place, it is noted that factors like decline in demand and obsolescence have a significant impact.

The pharmaceutical industry in india has the capability of producing a wide range of bulk drugs, covering a large spectrum of technologies and almost all formulations. In fact, the country is almost fully self-reliant in terms of formulation technology. In the case of bulk drugs, the technologies include those for sulpha drugs, vitamins, hormones and a number of new synthetic drugs like Flumequine, Pefloxacin, Ramipiril Ketorolac, Lisinopirl etc.

Among the bulk drugs which are critical to the country's health needs, the two most important ones are Penicillin and Rifampicin. The basic stage production of Penicillin and Rifampicin has been steadily growing and almost half of the country's demand for these two important drugs is met by indigenous production.

Two public sector undertakings, namely, Hindustan Antibiotics Limited (HAL) and Indian Drugs and Pharmaceuticals Limited (IDPL), account for almost 90 per cent of the Penicillin production in the Country. In addition to one private sector unit, which had commenced production of Penicillin in the last years, three more Penicillin manufacturing units in the private sector, with an investment of about Rs. 500 crore, are expected to commence commercial production in 1995. The indigenous production of Penicillin is thus expected to almost double from the existing level to meet the country's demand in the coming years.

In addition to the two manufactures of inermediates of Rifampicin from the basic stage, which today meets about 50 per cent of the indigenous demand of this important anti-TB and anti-leprosy drug, industrial license has been issued to another unit to produce this drug from the basic stage.

In view of the experience gained over the years, the Government had felt the need to modify the existing Drug Policy, 1986 so as to bring it in consonance with the Industrial Policy, 1991 and the present EXIM Policy as also to simplify and streamline the existing pricing system. The salient features of the Modifications in Drug Policy, 1986 announced on the 15 September 1994 are: (i)

Abolition of Industrial Licencing for all bulk drugs, their intermediates and formulations thereof except in case of five bulk drugs reserved for manufacture in the public sector and bulk drugs produced by the use of recombinant DNA technology as well as those requiring in-vivo use of nucleic acid as the active principles; (ii) Foreign investment upto 51 per cent will be automatically permitted in the case of all bulk drugs, their intermediates and formulations; (iii) automatic approval, as per the industrial policy, for foreign technology agreements shall be given in the case of all bulk drugs, their intermediates and formulations, except those produced by the use of recombinant DNA techology; (iv) Measures to give further impetus to R&D in the During Sector are as follows: (a) A new drug which has not been produced elsewhere, if developed through indigenous R&D would be put outside price control for a period of 10 years from the date of commercial production in favour of the Company who undertook the R&D; (b) The Department of Chemicals and Petrochemicals would set up an Inter-Ministerial group to decide, within a set time frame, on measures to give further impetus to R&D in the Drug Sector, and (c) The Ministry of Health and Family Welfare would further steamline the required procedures and steps for the quick-evaluation and clearance of new durg applications, specially those developed through indigenous R&D; (v) The system of price control would be operated through a single list of price controlled drugs, selected on the basis of transparent and objective criteria as laid down in the Modifications in Drug Policy, 1986" and formulations based thereon with a MAPE of 100 per cent; (vi) In case of basic manufacture, higher by four per cent over the existing rates which are 14 per cent on net worth or 22 per cent on capital employed; (vii) To achieve uniformity in prices of widely used formulations, it has been decided that there should be ceiling on prices for commonlymarketed standard pack sizes of price controlled formulations and that it would be obligatory for all, including small scale units, to follow the prices so fixed; (viii) An independent body of experts, to be called the National Pharmaceutical Pricing Authority, will be entrusted with the task of price-fixation/revision and other related medicines which are taken out of price control. In case, the prices of these medicines rise unreasonably, the Government would take appropriate measures, incluing reclamping of price control. (x) A National Drug Authority would be set up by an Act of the Parliament, to be steered by the Ministry of Health and Family Welfare, to look after the quality control aspects, rational use of drugs and related matters; and (xi) To provide better focus to all matters relating to development and promotion of indigenous and other system of medicines, a separate Department would be created by the Ministry of Health and Family Welfare.

The Drugs (Prices Control) Order (DPCO), 1995 has been notified by the Government on 6 January 1995. This Order has now come into force in place of the DPCO, 1987. The new DPCo has taken into account the modifications in the Drug Policy, 1986 announced by the Government in September 1994 in regared to the price control on drugs and has been issued in exercise of the powers conferred on the Central Government in September 1994 in regard to the price control on drugs and has been issued in exercise of the powers conferred on the Central Government by Section 3 of the Essential Commodities Act, 1955.

Seventy six drugs have been identified for being kept in the First Schedule of the DPCO which lists the drugs to be kept under price control. Unlike the DPCO, 1987 now there is a single list of drugs under price control with a Maximum Allowable Post Manufacturing Expenses (MAPE) of 100 per cent. Twenty two drugs, so far outside price control have been brought in the price controlled category. Some of these were having a heavy annual turnover exceeding Rs. 10 crore. Eighty three drugs have been decontrolled. Many of these were having an insignificant annual turnover with a declining usage or negligible growth.

With price control on the 76 drugs mentioned in Schedule-I of the DPCO almost 50 per cent of the retail pharmaceutical market would be under price control. The associations of drugs manufacturers have been cautioned to advise all their members to exercise restraint and self discipline in regard to medicines going out of price control and to ensure that their prices are not raised unreasonably, so that Government is not constrained to excercise its powers to bring back these medicines under price control.

It is envisaged that the list of drug to be kept under price control will be reviewed periodically, based on the data to be collected in this regard. Substantial changes have been brought about so as to make the reporting system by way of forms and information required to be submitted periodically by the Industry to the Government, less cumbersome.

An important provision introduced is the stipulation of time limits of two months for deciding applications for price revision of formulations and four months for price fixation/revision of applications regarding bulk drugs. There is also a stipulation in the DPCO enjoining the Government to notify on an annual basis the norms relating to conversion costs, packing material costs and packing charges.

The new DPCO also provides for fixing of ceiling prices for commonly used packs of formulations based on price controlled drugs and these prices would be applicable to all manufactures and also the single ingredient formultions sold under generic name. The small scale sector will not be required to come for price fixation for these packs and they will be required to only adhere to the discipline of observing the ceiling prices. In regard to the other packs they would continue to enjoy, as before, exemption from price control on formulations.

A provision has also been added in the DPCO to allow for exemption from price control to a new bulk drug, which has not been produced elsewhere if developed through indigenous R&D. Further a provision has also been built to allow the of use funds collected in the Drug Equilisation Account for the purpose of promoting higher education and research in pharmaceutical sciences and technology and purposes incidental thereto.

The DPCO 1995 lays down a more transparent procedure for the working of the price control mechanism, which would be in the ultimate interest of the consumers as well as the manufacturers.

About 250 units in the organised sector, five of these in the public sector (IDPL, HAL, SSPL, BCPL and BIL) and six in the joint sector, and about 5,000 units in the small scale sector are engaged in the production of drugs. Of these, more than 100 are engaged in the production of bulk drugs.

Indian Drugs and Pharmaceuticals Limited (IDPL) incorporated under the Companies Act, 1956 on 5 April 1961, is a premier undertaking. The company has five plants including two wholly-owned subsidiaries; one each located at Rishikesh (Uttar Pradesh), Hyderabad (Andhra Pradesh), Gurgaon (Haryana), Madras (Tamil Nadu) and Muzaffarpur (Bihar). IDPL is a major producer of antibiotics like Pencillin-G, Tetracycline, Oxytetracycline from the basic stages. It is a leading producer of Vitamins again from the basic stages. In Madras Plant (subsidiary), the company produces sufgical instruments and formulations.

The company has a fully equipped Research Centre at the Synthetic Drug Plant in Hyderabad. IDPL has also set-up three subsidiary companies in collaboration with the respective state governments for production of quality pharmaceutical formulations. Rajasthan Drugs and Pharmaceuticals Limited (RDPL), Jaipur (Rajasthan); Uttar Pradesh Drugs and Pharmaceuticals Limited (UPDPL), Lucknow (Uttar Pradesh) and Orissa Drugs and Chemicals Limited (ODCL), Bhubaneswar (Orissa).

Hindustan Antibiotics Limited (HAL) incorporated on 1 March 1954, was the first public sector undertaking in the field of pharmaceuticals. The company set-up primarily with the objective of manufacturing Penicillin and other antibiotics. It also produces streptomycin, gentamycin, haymycin and aurofungin, besides formulations.

The company has recently entered into MOU for a joint venture tie-up with MAX-GB Limited for upgradation of the Pencillin-G production facilities. HAL has three subsidiary companies promoted in collaboration with the respective state government-Karnataka Antibiotics and Pharmaceuticals Limited (KAPL), Bangalore (Karnataka); Maharashtra Antibiotics and Pharmaceuticals Limited (MAPL), Nagpuir (Maharashtra) and Manipur State Drugs and Pharmaceuticals Limited (MSDPL), Imphal (Manipur).

There are three public sector undertakings engaged in the manufacture of drugs and formulations located at Calcutta (West Bengal). These were private sector comapnies, poineers again in their own field, but had been ailing over the year for various reasons. The management of these companies were taken over by the Central Government in terms of the Industries (Development & Regulation) Act, 1951 and subsequently they were nationalised and new public sector companies were formed. Bengal Immunity Limited (BIL), Bengal Chemicals and Pharmaceuticals Limited (BCPL) and Smith Stanistreet Pharmaceuticals Limited (SSPL) are these three public sector undertakings with their main manufacturing activities concentrated in the State of West Bengal. BIl is one of the largest producers of SERA and vaccines toxoids.

It also produces other pharmaceutical formulations. BCPL with four manufacturing units, is the largest producer of anti-snake verum in India. It also produces chemicals like sulphuric acid, alum, chrome salts and home products like soaps, hair oil, perfumes etc. BCPL also produces herbal products. SSPL is engaged in the manufacture of pharmaceutical formulations.

The textile sector plays a vital role in the overall economy of the country. Textile exports account for over 30 per cent of the total exports from the country. The burgeoning growth in exports from the textile sector in the recent years has been one of the most striking features of India's economic development. The textile sector occupies a very prominent place in terms of employment generation.

The sectors like handloom, handicrafts, powerloom, sericulture and readymade * potential. The total employment in textile sector has risen from about 39 million during 1990-91 at about 47 million during 1994-95. The industry has witnessed a phenomenal growth during the last four decades. The spindleage increased from 11 million in 1951 to over 29.10 million and rotors from 45,000 in 1989 to 1,46,000 in 1994. The loomage, however has declined in the organised sector. Out of 1,227 cotton/man-made fibre textile mills, 187 mills are in public sector, 124 and 915 are in cooperative and private sectors respectively. Capacity utilisation in spinning sector of textile mills has increased from 69 per cent in 1985-86 to 84 per cent in 1993-94. However, the capacity utilisation in composite sector has declined from 62 per cent in 1985-86 to 54 per cent in 1993-94.

Research associations

Ahmadabad Textile Industry's Research Association, Ahmadabad, Bombay Textile Research Association, Bombay, South IndiaTextile Research Association, Coimbatore and Northern India Textile Research Association, Ghaziabad are four cotton textile research associations registered under the Societies Registration Act, 1860, and functioning under the adminstrative control of Ministry of Textile. The main objective of these institutions is to carry out research and render consultancy services (*i.e.* Quality Management Service-ISO 9000) to industry on various aspects of textile technology with a view to reducing the cost and improving the quality and durability of fabrics, reducing pollution, conserving energy and utilising waste, adopting new technology and improving the technologies in the decentralised handloom sector.

Silk and Art Silk Mills' Research Association (SASMIRA), Bombay is a textile research association registered under the Societies Registration Act 1860 (XXI of 1860) of Maharashtra State. Its headquarters are located at Bombay. The SASMIRA's principal activities included research and development, provision of technical services, testing and training facilities in the fields of silk and art-silk. Man-Made Textile Research Association (MANTRA) established in 1981, occupies a status of the leading R&D and educational institution in

India today. as one of the National Textile Research Laboratory, MANTRA caters to multifarious needs of textile and allied industry at large. Though activities of MANTRA are primarily aimed at planned and healthy growth of decentalised textile industry of south Gujarat, its impact beyond south Gujarat is also significant.

Indian Jute Industries' Resarch Association (IJIRA), Calcutta, registered under the West Bengal Societies Registration Act, 1961, is an autonomous cooperative research organisation under the administrative control of the Ministry of Textiles, Government of India.

The objective of IJIRA is to promote research and other scientific work connected with the jute trade and industries allied with or accessory thereto, to establish and maintain laboratories and foster education of persons engaged in or likely to be engaged in the said trade and industry, to encourage discoveries, to examine and publish information regarding the nature and merits of inventions, improvements, materials and designs connected with the said trades or industries.

The Jute Industry in the country is traditionally export oriented. India ranks number one in raw jute and jute goods production and number two in export of jute goods in the world. Jute packaging materials are facing tough challenges from other low priced synthetic substitutes. As a measure to use jute in non-packaging sectors, Government has undertaken a number of steps for diversification.

The most significant aspect of the diversification programme is the UNDP assisted National Jute Programme under which an assistance of the order of US dollar 230 lakh from UNDP is being utilised by providing matching input from Government of India. A large number of projects covering the areas of raw jute production, R&D, product development, human resource development, and marketing are under imnplementation. To fulfil these objectives, the National Centre for Jute Diversification is being set up.

In the silk sector, Government has made an allocation of Rs. 901 crore for development of sericulture during Eighth Plan. The employment generation during this period is targeted at 10.50 lakh persons which would bring the accumulated employment under the sericulture sector to 65 lakh persons by 1997. The employment in silk sector during 1994-95 is anticipated to be 61 lakh persons as against 50 lakh persons in 1993-94. During 1994-95, the silk sector has exceeded its export target of Rs. 837.31 crore by 12.8 per cent.

The handloom industry is an important sector which provides employment to about 12 million people and contributes over 20 per cent of total cloth production. Production of handloom cloth also increased from 4,295 million sq mtr. during 1990-91 to 6,028 million sq. mtr. during 1994-95 showing an annual increase of about 10.1 per cent. In order to further increase production and generate additional employment opportunities in the handloom sector during 1992-93, a scheme was introduced to develop 3,000 handloom development centres and 500 quality dyeing units which will benefit 30 lakh weavers till September 1995.

Already 122 Handloom Development Centres and 45 Quality Dyeing Centres have been set up. An Integrated Village Handloom Development Scheme, project package scheme and National Silk Yarn Bank scheme have been launched between 1991-95 with an outlay of Rs. 63 crore and Rs. 20 crore respectively for the Eighth Plan period. A project on development of handloom products using jute fibre titled 'Development and Transfer for Technology for use of Jute Fibre in Handloom Textiles' was sanctioned by the Government during 1993-94 with an outlay of about Rs. 10.30 crore. Beside, a scheme for setting up jute handloom development centres has been introduced in January 1995.

Export of cotton handloom textiles amounted to Rs. 1,229 crore (US dollar 392 million) in April-December 1994 against Rs. 911 crore (US dollar 291 million) achieved in April-December 1993, thereby registering an increase of 34.8 per cent both in rupee and dollar terms.

In the decentralised powerloom sector which contributes over 70 per cent of the total cloth production, new scheme to set up computer aid designing centres (CADs) in the area of powerloom concentration has been inroduced. The aim of such centres is to upgrade the existing quality and design of cloth production by the decentralised powerloom sector so as to enable the powerloom fabric to compete in the international market in an effective fashion. Two such centres have been established at Sholapur (Maharashtra) and Coimbatore (Tamil Nadu). Remaining five centres are under process of being set up.

Textile exports, including handicraft, jute and coir, presently account for about 37 per cent of India's total exports as against of 35 per cent during the previous year. There has been a significant increase in exports from the textile sector including jute, coir and handicrafts have grown from the level of Rs. 9,932 crore during 1990-91 to Rs. 31,644 crore during 1994-95.

The Final Act of the Uruguay Round of GATT negotiations has been signed by 111 countries at the Minsterial Conference in Marrakesh on 15 April 1994. The agreement on textile and clothing which forms a part of the Final Act, signalled the end of the Multi-Fibre Agreement (MFA) era, in which discriminatory restraints were put by the developed countries on the exports of textiles by developing countries like India. The World Trade Organisation has consequently come into existence w.e.f. 1 January 1995. During the next 10 years the multi-fibre agreement would be phased out and in the different stages the quotas will be removed. The agreement is expected to boost textile exports in the coming years.

In order to provide systematic training to our fashion designers and help them compete in the international market in an effective manner, in addition to the existing National Institute of Fashion Technology (NIFT) centre at New Delhi, five more new NIF centres have been opened at Bombay, Hyderabad, Calcutta, Madras and Gandhi Nagar.

Handicrafts constitute an important segment of the decentralised sector of our economy and provides employment to over six million artisans, roughly 1/5th of the total household industries scatteed throughout the country especially in rural and semi-urban areas.

The Office of the Development Commissioner for Handicrafts implements Plan schemes covering various areas like training, design, development, technology upgradation, market promotion, exhibition and publicity exports etc. Export of handicrafts including hand-knitted carpets during 1994-95 was recorded at Rs. 4,458 crore as compared to Rs. 3,360 crore during 1993-94. The employment in the handicraft sector has increased increased to 64.2 lakh persons during 1994-95.

Special programmes have been launched to promote embroidery, *zari* and *zardosi* costume jewellery and imitation jewellery for both in the domestic and international market as a measure to generate more employment opportunity for crafts people. Besides, a UNDP assisted programme has been undertaken to promote wood based handicrafts for exports. *Kaleen* label has been introduced by Carpet Export Promotion Council (CEPC) to be fixed on the carpets for export as a hall-mark of commitmemt towards complete eradication of child labour from the Indian carpet industry and contribution towards welfare of children and carpet weavers. A country-wide census has been launched for the first time to collect information about the handicrafts artisans. This will help in building up the data base for this sector.

The manufacture of all types of automobile vehicles is delicensed. There has been a significant growth in the production of automotive vehicles during 1994-95 as compared to that in 1993-94 * has been 1,94,999 as against 1,41,436 in 1993-94. Production of cars has gone up from 2,09,695 in 1993-94 to 2,64,007 in 1994-95. * The production of three-wheelers has gone up from 91,608 in 1993-94 to 1,27,532 in 1994-95. During 1994-95, the production of tractors was 1,62,900 as compared to 1,36,581 in 1993-94.

Sixty one units in the organised sector are manufacturing soap with an installed capacity of 6,60,772 tonnes per year. Production of soap in this sector was of the order of 3,40,366 tonnes during 1993-94 and 3,35,125 tonnes during 1994-95. There are 26 units in organised sector for manufacturing of synthetic detergents with an installed capacity of 6,05,000 tonnes per annum. Production of detergents was 3,07,738 tonnes during 193-94 and 3,09,738 tonnes during 1994-95.

Leather is a highly labour-oriented industry in India and has been identified as one of the major thrust areas for export. The export performance of leather sector has been improving considerably over the last 3-4 years. The value of export of leather and leather products went up from Rs. 3,693 crore during 1992-93 to Rs. 4,139.3 crore in

1993-94. In the year 1994-95, the export from this sector was to the tune of Rs. 5,000 crore (provisionally), showing a growth rate of nearly 18 per cent over the last year. Footwear in the leather sector has been identified as an area of extreme focus for exports and in 1993-94 leather footwear and footwear components valued at Rs. 1,481.3 crore have been exported.

A National Leather Development Programme (NLDP) with UNDP assistance of the order of US dollar 15.05 million and Government inputs of Rs. 28.43 crore is currently being implemented by the Government for integrated development of the leather industry through the selected institutions/agencies in the country. The duration of the programme is four years and it has started its operations in June 1992 in accordance with the Work Plan. The Programme covers, *inter-alia,* areas such as human resources development, improving support services, pollution control and enhancement of exports.

The Programme has already been able to establish linkages with some of the most reputed international organisations, such as AFPIC and MCT, Melbourne, in the areas of education and training. The Indian institutions have been able to upgrade the training systems for design and manufacture of footwear, garments and asserted leather products. The leather sector units in the country can directly seek assistance by the selected institutions on software.

The areas earmarked for assistance are human resource development, product development, development of supporting industries (components, machinery), marketing etc. A market research unit which has been established at Council for Leather Exports, Madras has commenced services. Resource Centre and Publication of bi-monthly *"World Leather Times"* has been started.

Chemical indusdry plays a pivotal role in the Indian economy. The Industry in India is well established and has witnessed rapid growth in the organic and inorganic sectors. The rate of growth of the chemical sector has consistently been higher than the average growth rate of the Indian industry. During the last decade (1981-82 to 1991), the industry has been averaging a growth rate of about 10 per cent per annum.

The present annual turnover in the chemical sector in India is estimated to be around Rs. 35,000-Rs. 40,000 crore which is likely to be doubled by the end of the century. In order to promote this highly technology oriented industry, a number of incentives have been given to promote development activities. With the liberalisation policy of the Indian economy, major reforms have been taken up in the Indian chemical industry.

Except for a small list of hazardous chemicals, all chemical items can be manufactured in India without requiring any industrial licensing. Even where licensing exists, the procedures have been streamlined. Entrepreneurs are, therefore, now free to set up chemical industries, by intimating to the Government through the Industrial Entrepreneurs Memorandum.

Development of organic chemical industry in India had started in April 1950, based on ethyl alcohol, manufactured from fermentation and distillation of sugarcane molasses and benezene available as a coke-oven by-product. At present, a substantial part of the industry is based on feedstock derived from petroleum. Basic organic chemicals like phenol, methanol, formaldehyde, acetone and acetic acid are manufactured in the country in substantial quantities. Major inorganic chemicals like soda ash, carbon black, calcium carbide, red phosphorous and potassium chlorates are all manufactured in the country and a position of near self-dufficiency has been achieved in all these chemicals. Alcohol producing industry was started in 1940 mainly to utilise molasses produced from fugar factories. With the growth of alcohol-based chemical industry in 1950's, production of alcohol has assumed importance in its own right.

Oil crisis has revived interest in the use of renewable feedstock like alcohol. It is mainly in India that a wide-range of organic chemical products are manufactured on a commercial scale with alcohol as the feedstock. The major downstream products made from ethyl alcohol (industrial alcohol) are acetic acid, acetic anhydride, acetone, butanol ethylacetate, polythene, styrene, PVC and synthetic rubber.

In keeping with the policy of economic liberalisation the price and movement control on molasses and alcohol have been removed with effect from 10 June 1993. This would ensure maximum utilisation of capacity in both the alcohol manufacturing sector and the sector utilising alcohol for downstream products like acetic acid, acetic anhydride etc.

Moreover, this is likely to improve the viablity of the sugar units who may be able to pay better prices for sugarcane to farmers. State governments are being persuaded for implementation of the policy of decontrol in their states.

In order to check undue increase in prices of industrial alcohol, customs duty on import of denatured alcohol has been reduced to 10 per cent with effect from 20 October 1993. Customs duty on molasses also has been reduced to 10 per cent with effect from 1 April 1995.

Dyestuff industry provides important inputs to many consuming industries contributing to the national economy. It is capable of meeting most of the local demands. In the organised sector, the industry is self-sufficient in terms of most of the inputs. There are around 50 units in the organised sector having a total installed capacity of 36,700 tonnes per annum against which the production achieved during 1993-94 was 31,100 tonnes.

The production for various classes of dyestuffs in 1994-95 is estimated to 31,600 tonnes. A large quantity of dyes and dye-intermediates is being exported and valuable foreign exchange being earned in this sector.

The industry contributes about 10 per cent of the total exports. The exports in the chemical sector have gone up from a level of around Rs. 1,600 crore in the year 1990-91 to around Rs. 3,600 crore in 1993-94, registering an increase of about 120 per cent.

Pesticides including insecticides, fungicides, weedicides, etc., are used extensively in agriculture and public health. The pesticide industry in india has made impressive progress and more than 60 technical grade pesticides are being successfully manufactured in the country. At present, more than 125 units are engaged in the manufacture of these technical grade pesticides and over 500 units are making pesticides formulations. As a result of the increased production of pesticides in the country, import of technical grade pesticides has come down considerably.

The estimated production of technical pesticides during 1994-95 is over 85,800 mt from an annual installed capacity of 1.25 lakh mt. As compared to this, the production during 1993-94 was around 85,600 mt.

In order to use the idle capacity available with pesticide units, the country has been able to enter the competitive field of export of pesticides. During 1992-93, the country has exported pesticides valued at Rs. 168.7 crore. This has increased to Rs. 261.24 crore during 1993-94. The courtry has started producing some new pesticides but continue to import their intermediates in the absence of technology for producing them.

Efforts are being made to acquire the right technology to manufacture intermediates for pesticides like Butachlor, Enosulfan etc. Till 1987-88, country was not able to export chemicals in larger quantities because of high cost of production of chemicals in India as compared to international prices. However, due to upgradation of technology and support given by the Government for exports, the Indian chemical industry have shown an impressive performance in the field of exports. During 1992-93, the export of chemical touched Rs. 3,475.5 crore.

There are two public sector units, namely, Hindustan Organic Chemicals Limited (HOCL) and Hindustan Insecticies Limited (HIL) in the chemical sector HOCL was incorporated in December, 1960 at Rasayani, Raigad district, Maharashtra, with the main objective of manufacturing chemical intermediates required for the manufacture of drugs, dyestuffs, rubber chemicals and laminates etc.

The company has two units; one each at Rasayani (Maharashtra) and Cochin (Kerala). Rasayani Unit produces organic grup of heavy chemical and intermediates such as nitrobenzene, hydrogen, aniline, sulphuric acid, acetic acid etc. Cochin unit produces phenol, acetone and propylene.

The company has floated a subsidiary company called Hindustan Fluocarbons Limited for setting up polytetraflurethylene (PTFE) plant in Medak district of Andhra Pradesh. HIL, incorporated in 1954, has at present three units at Delhi, Udyogamandal (Kerala) and

Rasayani (Maharashtra). The company als has a subsidiary Hyderabad and a factory at Kovur. HIL is engaged in the manufacture of DDT, BHC, malathion, endosulfan and butachlor, the five major pesticides used in the country. Monocrotophos Plant has also been commissional last year and is in operation

Attainment of industrialisation over the last 48 years has been striking feature of Indian economic development process which was launched as a conscious and deliberate policy in the early fifties. In pursuance of this policy, large investment has been made in building up capacity over a wide spectrum of industries. Industrial production has made rapid strides in terms of variety, quality and quantity.

There has been a substantial diversification of industrial base during this period with the consequent ability to produce a very broad range of industrial goods. Self-reliance has been achieved in basic and capital good. Indigenous capabilities have now been established to the point of virtual self-sufficiency so that further expansion in various sectors such as mining, irrigation, power chemicals, transport and communication can be based primarily on indigenous equipment.

Process of industrialisation has also fostered entrepreneurship and development of a wide variety of technical, managerial and operative skills. Today, the country is in a position to provide consultancy services as well as managers, technicians and skilled workers for setting up industrial projects aborad.

The Industrial Policy Resolution of 1948 marked the beginning of the evolution of Indian Industrial Policy. The resolution not only defined the broad contours of the policy, it delineated the role of the State in the industrial development both as an entrepreneur and as an authority.

Successive policy resolutions also reiterated this basic tilt in favour of the public sector. The Industrial Policy Resolution of 1956 gave the public sector a strategic role in the economy. It categorised industries which would be the exclusive responsibility of state or would progressively come under state control and others. Earmarking the pre-eminent position to the public sector, it envisaged private sector co-existing with the State and thus attempted to give the policy framework flexibility.

The Industrial Policy initiatives undertaken by Government since July 1991 have been designed to build on the past industrial achievements and to accelerate the process of making Indian industry internatinally competitive. It recognises the strength and maturity of the industry and attempts to provide the competitive stimulus for higher growth. The thrust of these initiatives has been to increase domestic and external competition through extensive application of market mechanism and facilitating forging of dynamic relationships with foreign investors and suppliers of technology. The process of reform has been continuous.

As on 31 March 1993 there were 245 central public sector undertakings, comprising of eight in the construction sector, 72 in services and remaining 165 in the manufacturing. The number of CPSUs as indicated above exclude nine companies, six insurance companies and three financial institutions with Central Government investment but without direct responsibility of management.

The total capital employed in the 245 CPSUs increased from Rs. 1,179.91 billion in 1991-92 to Rs. 1,399.33 billion in 1992-93. The overall rate of return on capital employed in the PSUs also increased from 2.0 per cent in 1991-92 to 2.43 per cent in 1992-93.

The number of small scale units as at the end of 31 March 1994 were 2.38 million comprising of 1.77 million registered units and 0.61 un-registered. The overall production in the small scale sector during 1993-94 has been estimated to have reached Rs. 2,416.5 billion. The total value of exports of these units has been Rs. 177.85 billion in 1992-93.

Industrialization

India has made rapid strides in industrialization, and today is one of the ten most industrialized nations of the world. But industrialization, as in the rest of the world, has brought with it unwanted and unanticipated consequences. These include unplanned urbanization, pollution and risk of accidents. Industrialization moreover not only affects the immediate environment, but has consequences for a larger region whose resources get intimately tied to new industrial development.

Yet as the country continues to industrialize and new plants come up, some of the underlying issues remain. Dirty industries continue moving South. Hazardous chemicals are dumped or brought for reprocessing to developing countries. Often, in developed countries, different values are attached to human life in the North and in the South. Different standards are applied, and processes and factories being discarded in developed countries get relocated in the developing ones.

The Bhopal disaster, when methyl isocyanate crept into the houses of sleeping residents on the morning of 3 December, 1984, killing over 3,000 people and maiming countless others for life, brought many of these issues into sharp focus. It was a tragic testimony of just how much could go wrong. The hazardous side of industry became painfully apparent to countless people in India and abroad. It questioned location policies, safety requirements of industries, the responsibilities of North-based multinational corporations, the preparedness for dealing with disasters, citizens' right to know about the industrial process and the risks involved.

Near the industries, water and air pollution problems are very serious. Water pollution not only affects surface water but also groundwater. It is estimated that 70 per cent of India's surface water is seriously polluted and 80 per cent of the population does not have access to safe drinking water. For instance in Patancheru in Andhra Pradesh, over 60 factories—most of them chemical units—discharge their toxic wastes into freshwater streams. In Bichhri in Rajasthan, chemical effluents from textile and chemical industries pollute the waters of rivers and wells.

The health impact of such cases is serious and the incidence of cancer, lung and skin diseases, and deformities is high in these areas. While they are restricted in extent, air pollution levels are high in industrial areas. For instance the average levels of particulate matter in the four metropolitan cities exceeds 360 mg/m while the WHO standard is 150 mg/m.

Another concern relates to occupational health incertain industries. Asbestosis, byssinosis and pneumonoconiosis are some of the occupational diseases reported. Silicosis has been reported in mines and other industries.

Several central and state statues, such as the Industrial Development Act, the Labour Acts, the Factories Act and the Municipal Acts have environmental provisions in them. However it was the enactment of the Water (Prevention and Control of Pollution) Act, 1974, and the Air (Prevention and Control of Pollution) Act, 1981, which made these environmental factors the principal object of legislation. The Bhopal tragedy caused a surge in environmental legislation and an umbrella Environment (Protection) Act was passed in 1986. This covers hazardous activities in addition to pollution.

Under the Environment (Protection) Act, 1986, the Central Government is responsible for laying down procedures and safeguards for handling hazardous substances. Rules have been made for the manufactures, storage and import of hazardous chemicals, their management and handling, as well as for the manufacture, use, import and storage of micro-organisms and genetically engineered organisms. Radioactive waste disposal is controlled through a regulatory board managed by the Bhabha Atomic Research Centre. The Government has also established a Central Crises Group Alert System with a control room at New Delhi to deal with major chemical accidents in the country.

Many industries and large projects need environmental clearance. The State Pollution Control Boards monitor industrial areas. The Government of India has made it mandatory to assess the environmental impact of new large undertaking in the country. The impact assessment covers not only air, water and soil polluiton, but also damage to historical monuments, wildlife, forests, and to natural resources in general. Unique to India is the recently enacted Mandatory Public Liability Insurance which makes it imperative for units dealing with hazardous substances to take insurance cover against damage to health or property of the community in the vicinity of the industry.

Industrial location policy is a crucial element in determining the impact of industry on the environment. Unplanned industrial growth has in some cases led to industrail conglomerates and urban sprawl. This has often led to prime agricultural and forest land being diverted for urban and industrial use. Near forests, urban areas have led to deforestation. For certain industries, a two-stage clearance procedure has been adopted by the Ministry of Environment and Forests, considering the site specific nature.

While legislation today has enabled authorities to step in, this alone cannot lead to improved environment in and around industries. For this to happen public awareness, as well as awareness and concern among the decision-makers is required. Where people have been consicous they have protested and not let polluting industries spoil their environment. Where industries have been conscious they have got together and taken initiatives for effluent treatment. A typical example of joint efforts by industry in the safe disposal of effluents is the Baroda Effluent Channel in Gujarat, managed by the Gujarat Industrial Development Corporation.

There is urgent need to create widespread awareness. Towards this end the Ministry of Environment and Forests has made a beginning by introducing a scheme for an Ecomark to lable environment-friendly products. NGOs too have several programmes to create environmental consciouness. School programmes to involve students in environmental quality monitoring have begun.

But finally environmental factors will only be taken into account where alternatives are availabel. Today with Indai opening up its economy to greater internationl participation in the industrialization of the country, it si important to ensure that the best and cleansest technologies are available for htis growth, so that industrialization occurs with the minimum of negative consequences.

In a wide spectrum of industry and agriculture and the entire gamut of services, there has been great progress in the country during the post-Independence era. The growth in several sectors have indeed been spectacular and in several others it has been modest while in a few others outright dismal. On Monday, 10 November 1996, the foundation stone for the automobile plant of the Hyundai Motor Company of South Korea, was laid at Irungattukottai, some 40 km from Chennai. The plant involves an outlay of $ 700 million (around Rs. 2500 crore) in the first phase; and another $ 400 million (around Rs. 1440 crore) in the second phase.

A production capacity of around 100,000 passenger cars in the 1300 cc-1500 cc range is envisaged. The first car is expected to roll out of the assembly line by October 1998. Most importantly, HMC promises a 70 per cent indigenous content from the first car. Which means prospects for dozens of additonal collaboration arrangements and investments for the production of components. At full production, the turnover of HMC will be in the region of Rs. 6000 crore.

This is the third mega investment in the automobile sector involving outlays exçeeding Rs. 1500 crore each. The other two relate to the Mahinndra-Ford India Ltd. project to produce passenger cars of similar capacity and in same medium segment; and by Ashok Leyland Ltd., planning to invest on facilities to expand capacity to 100,000 commercial vehicles.

In recent months total investments promised in Tamil Nadu exceed Rs. 5000 crore–an outlay that perhaps exceed all investments made on new projects in the first instance all through the past 50 years.

In all these areas, and in a wide spectrum of industry and agriculture and the entire gamut of services, there has been great progress through the years of Independent India. The growth in several sectors have indeed been spectacular and in several others, it had been modest; and in a few others outright dismal. The bench-making has been done both in regard to the potential offered by India and by developments in several other countries which started on industrialisation much later than we did. South Korea offers a ready example.

In looking at growth, over the last five decades, we can segment these into five distinct phase that roughly correspond with decennial slots.

In accordance with the prevailing thinking, the First Five year Plan stated that the objective of industrial planning was to make good the deficiencies in production of key industrial items and to initiated development, which would enable cumulative expansion of such basic production.

There was better appreciation in the First Plan of the need for coordination of industrial planning with the formulation of other economic policies, such as customs and excise tariff structure, import and export policy, investment and technology policy and monetary and financial policy. The Second Plan and later plans have been encreasingly concerned with the allocation of public resources and much less with indications and policies to direct the whole economy indesired directions.

The Industrial Policy Statement of 1973, inter alia, identified high-priority industries where investment from large industrial houses and foreign companies would be permitted. The Industrial Policy Statement of 1980 focussed attention on the need for promoting competition in domestice market, technological upgradation and modernisation. The policy laid the foundation for an increasingly competitive export base and for encouraging foreign investment in high priority technology areas. This found expression in the Sixth Five Year Plan, which emphasised the need for productivity to be the central concern in all economic and production activities.

Nevertheless the sector continued to provide the thrust for the development of heavy industries. In critical areas such as power, railways, coal, petroleum, steel and fertilisers, the public sector has been intensely involved in setting the pace of development.

Apart from public investments in basic industry and infrastructure, the expansion of the private sector in line with Plan objectives and priorities were greatly facilitated by financial institutions. An elaborate network of specialised development banking institutions with the Industrial Development Bank of India at the apex was established to help finance industrial investment in the private sector. These institutions, numbering over 50, have become the major source of long-term finance for the corporate sector.

As the statement on Industrial Policy, 1991 says, "These policies created a climate for rapid industrial growth in the country. Thus on the eve of the Seventh Five year Plan, a broad-based infractructure had been built up. Basic industries had been established. A high degree of self-reliance in a large number of items–raw materials, intermediates, finished goods—had been achieved. New growth centres of industrial activity had emerged, as had a new generation of entrepreneurs. A large number of engineers, technicians and skilled workers has been trained."

The Sixth Plan had achieved augmentation of new capacity more or less in consonance with the targets in alarge number of insdustries including, among others, aluminium, zinc, lead thermoplastics, yarn, petrochemical intermediates, electrical equipment, cement and consumer durables. However shortfall in production had taken place in some basic industries, such as steel, cement, non-ferrous metals, fertilisers and certain other industries, including textiles, jute manufactures, sugar, drugs and pharmaceuticals, commercial vehicles and railway wagons. Production targets were exceed in a few industries like machine toos, passenger cars, motor cycles and scooters, consumer electronics and communication equipment. Domestic imbalances resulting from shortfalls in production hasd to be corrected through imports of essential commodities, like steel, cement, fertilisers and sugar.

A technological thrust was given during the Plan period in certain industries in the engineering sector. The first 500 MW thermal generating unit was commissioned and the manufacture of 500 MW turbo generators and boilers had commenced. There has been a systematic upgradation of production technology for other equipment, needed by the power sector. The manufacture of equipment for 1350 tonnes per day fertiliser units and blast furnaces of 3200 cubic metres capacity for steel plants was being undertaken in the country. A strong base had been laid for the rapid development of the electronics sector.

The Seventh Plan recognised the need to consolidate on these strengths and to take initiatives to prepare Indian industry to respond effectively to the emerging challenges.

A number of policy and procedural changes which were introduced in 1985-86 aimed at increasing productivity, reducing costs and improving quality. Production capacity restrictions on the industries were gradually reduced and broad banding, which enabled a manufacturer to choose and produce any product mix which suited him in the context of the prevailing market conditions was introduced. In 1986, as against a policy of re-endorsement of existing capacity, the scheme of minimum economic scale of production was introduced with Letters of Intent prescribing a minimum economic size for a single unit. The accent was on opening the domestic market to increased competition and readying the industry to stand on its own in the face of international competition. The public sector was freed from a number of constraints and given a large measure of autonomy. The technological and managerial modernisation of industry was pursued as the key instrument for increasing productivity and improving competitiveness in the world.

As a result of the policies pursued since Independence, the long term trend of industrial growth for over forty years since 1950 is a trend annual growth of just over 6 per cent. This, says rakesh MOhan in an essay in Bimal Jalan's book on Indian Economy, "is quite an achievement, given the magnitude of distortions built into the system." He divides the growth record into three distinct periods: 7.7 per cent annual growth over the first three plan periods (1950-1965), four per cent annual growth over the holiday (1966-69) and the Fourth and Fifth Plan periods (1969-79), and finally the recovery to about 7.7 per cent growth over the Sixth and Seventh periods.

The period 1966-1980, says Mohan is effectively the dark period for Indian economy. This period encompassed a number of exogenous shocks: the devastating three-year drought of 1965-68, the aftermath of increased defence espenditures resulting from 1962 was with China and two wars with Pakistan, the oil price shocks of 1973 and 1979, and the downturn in the availability of foreign resources. During this period, the Indian economy was constantly struggling to adjust.

As a result of policy changes, the composition of

Indian industry had undergone great transformation. At Independence, the consumer goods industry accounted for almost half of all industrial production. In 1991 such industries accounted for only about 20 per cent. In contrast, capital goods production was less than 4 per cent of total industrial production. In 1991, it had gone up to 24 per cent. Similarly basic goods share had increased from 20 per cent to 40 per cent.

As per the quick estimates of the Index of Industrial Production, the overall growth of industrial production during April-June 1996 was 8.5 per cent over the corresponding period of 1995 with the following sectoral contributions. As per the use based classificaton of industries, the overall growth has been broad based. After being relatively sluggish in the last two years, Intermediate Goods have recorded a growth of 11.9% in April-June 1996.

Industrial performance based on the production of 172 industries which together have a weight of 88% of IIP indicate a growth of 9.98 per cent in April-June, 1996. There has been deceleration in the growth of certain core sectors such as electricity, crude petroleum, steel, fertilizers, ferro alloys, jute manufacturers etc.

The first five months of the current financial year witnessed a sharp drop in the growth rate of infrastructure industries to 3.5% from 7.8% for the corresponding period of 1995-96. Amongst the industries that declined are: crude petroleum at (-)10.4% from 7.2%, electricity at 2.4% from 8.2% and saleable steel at 4.6% from 8.5%.

The performance of six Infrastructure Industries which is a critical indicator of the overall health.

The Office of Economic Adviser (OEA) also collects advance information on the production of 24 selected industries which have a weight of around 50% in the IIP. According to the information available, these industries have recorded a growth of 5.8% during April-July, 1996.

As per the information provided by CMIE, the corporate sector recorded a robust 22% growth in sales during 1995-96. This was particularly impressive because it comes after an unsually high increase of 23% recorded during 1994-95. The growth was reasonably well spread over major industry groups. In particular, the automobiles group, the chemicals sector and machinery industry performed exceptionally well.

About a quarter of the companies surveyed recorded sales growth rates less than 10%. At the same time, a little over a quarter of the companies recorded growth rates of more than 50%. Growth was mostly concentrated amongst companies with a size of Rs.75 crore to Rs.100 crore in terms of sales.

Interest payment by the corporate sector increased at a faster pace (nearly 24%) compared to the growth in sales. High interest cost during the year adversely affected most companies except the very large ones. However, the higher interest cost did not dampened sales growth in 1995-96.

According to the report of the RPG Foundation, the performance of non-finance companies was the highest during 1995-96 when compared to the other years in the 90s. Despite the liquidity crunch, the companies fared well mainly due to high and relatively inelastic demand for industrial goods, increased velocity of circulation of money, better inventory management and a decline in the incremental capital output ratio of the corporate sector. Thus despite paying a higher interest of at least 3% points more, there was a marginal improvemeant in the average rate of capital employed and the net profitability of the corporate sector.

Advance indications of the corporate performance for the first half of 1996-97 are now becoming available. These indicate a slow down in sales growth to around 9 per cent compared to over 24 per cent in the previous year. With inflation at around 5 per cent, real sales growth is around 4-5 per cent. Inventory levels are also increasing and with that interest burden. The liquidity crunch witnessed in 1995-96 and resultant high interest rates are affecting corporate investment in the current year.

In a period of weak sales growth, one normally excepts a high inventory holdings. However, continued high interest rates in last few years has resulted in better inventory management and the inventory levels have been declining continuously. These were around 20 per cent of sales in 1995-96. Even a significant increase in inventory holdings will not make much difference to the production levels.

NCAER regularly conducts a Survey of Industrial Confidence. According to the latest information available the business confidence index for August has sharply declined indicating that second half of 1996-97 may be even worse than the first half. Psychologically the corporate sector is now excepting a slow down in industrial activity and the inertia of this deceleration may result in a slow down greater than what economic fundamental may indicate.

Power sector

Power generation during 1995-96 at 380.1 billion kwh recorded a growth of 8.3 per cent over 1994-95. Total generation of power during April-November, 1996 at 257.2 billion kwh, compared to 248.7 billion kwh during April-November, 1995 recorded a growth of 3.4 per cent. While thermal and nuclear generation went up by 6.5 per cent and 4.1 per cent respectively, hydro generation declined by 7.7 per cent. Owing to the low Plant Load Factor (PLF) of thermal plants, heavy Transmission and Distribution (T&D) losses and other operational and technical inefficiencies, full benefits are not being derived even from existing capacities.

Thermal plants at present account for 74 per cent of total power generation and hydro electricity plants 24 per cent, with the balance 2 per cent being generated by nuclear plants. The installed capacity of power generation as on March 31, 1996 was 83,288 MW. During the first 4 years of the 8th plan (1992-97) capacity addition has been 14,799 MW as against the 8th Plan target of 30,858 MW. About 12 per cent of the total capacity addition during the first four years has been accounted for by hydro and the remaining by thermal units

Nearly half of the addition to capacity occurred in the Central Sector. 4.25 per cent was accounted for by the State Sector and the rest in the Private Sector. While the Central Sector has achieved 57.0 per cent of the 8th Plan, the State and Private Sectors achieved 42.3 per cent and 41.9 per per cent respectively. During the period (April-November) of the current year (1996-97) there has been a capacity addition of 53.460 MW of which 105.60 MW is in the private sector.

Several reasons have been identified for slippages in capacity creation in the Central and State sector. These include paucity of funds, delay in placement of order for main plant and equipment, delay in supply of equipment by suppliers, procedural delays in land acquisition, non-resolution of inter-state disputes, problems due to disturbed site conditions at some of the projects, unresolved issues in fuel linkages, suspension of work due to contract failures and resettlement and rehabilitation problems. Another important reason for slippages, particularly in State sector projects has been that the States saw the announcement of policy for private participation as an opportunity to cut back on their involvement in generation projects. As a result many projects that were scheduled for commissioning through the State sector resources have not been provided adequate funds for timely completion.

The PLF is an important indicator of operational efficiency of thermal power plants. The average PLF in the Central PSUs in 1995-96 and in April-November, 1996 was appreciably higher than that achieved by the State Electricity boards (SEBs). The low capacity utilisation of thermal power plants of the SEBs is largely due to deficiencies in management and operation, lack of proper maintenance and non-availabilty of coal of appropriate quality. There were wide inter-state variations in the average PLF of thermal plants and the average PLF in the case of Eastern and North Eastern regions continued to be much lower than the all India average during. 1996-97.

An action plan has been drawn up to improve the performace of the power sector in a phased manner. This involves short-term, medium-term and long-term measures and covers both the physical and financial aspects of generation, transmission and distribution of power. Short-term measures include overhaul and maintenance (O & M) of boileers and optimal operation of the regional grids. Significant improvements in the PLF of thermal power stations can be effected through medium-term measures like proper maintenance planning. In the long-term, the availability factor of the older thermal power plants can be improved by appropriate renovation and modernisation (R & M) programmes.

In the power sector, SEBs are responsible for distribution to all end users other than a small segment under the purview of privae distribution companies. As a result, in principle, all the electricity generated is to be sold to SEBs. But the financial condition of SEBs, though it differs from one state to the other is fragile in most cases. The magnitude of losses incurred by SEBs over the period 1990-91 to 1994-95.

The industry and agriculture sectors continued to be the two most important categories of consumers in terms of their relative shares, with SEB electricity charges set at much below the unit cost for the agricultural sector and above the unit cost for the industrial sector. In none of the SEBs does unit revenue realisation from the agricultural sector cover even a reasonable fraction of the unit average cost for the SEB, and this is leading to heavy financial losses.

The commercial losses of SEBs which, in absolute terms, were a little over Rs. 4.000 crore in 1991-92, have shot up over a five year period to Rs. 10,941 crore in 1996-97 (RE). The hidden subsidy for the agriculture and domestic sectors has increased from Rs. 7,248 crore in 1991-92 to Rs. 19,227 crore in 1996-97 (RE) and is projected to further go upt to Rs. 21,580 crore in 1997-98. Introduction of proposed national minimum agricultural tariff of 50 paise/kwh, even if implemented, will leave uncovered a substantial proportion of the subsidy provided to the sector.

In addition the SEBs have continued to suffer from high T & D losses, which stood at 21.8 per cent in 1992-93, have come down marginally to 20.9 per cent in 1994-95. These figures are very high when compared with the international average of less than 10 per cent for the advanced countries of the world. A reduction in T & D losses by 1 per cent would result in saving of capacity of about 800 MW at present day consumption. These T & D losses are due to the sparsely distributed loads over large rural area, substancial amount of energy sold at low voltage level. under-investment in the power distribution systems, inadequated billing and high pilferage. Inherent losses in conductors and equipment can be brought down through system improvement schemes and the pilferage and theft of energy can be reduced through appropriate administrative measures.

Restoration of the financial health of SEBs and improvement in their operational performance continue to remain the most crucial issues in the power sector. In terms of Section 59 of the Electricity (Supply) Act, 1948, SEBs are required to earn a minimum rate of return (ROR) of 3 per cent on their net fixed assest in service, after providing for depreciation and interest charges. This provision was to become operative from the accounting year of 1985. However the SEBs are yet to comply with this statutory stipulation. Whereas in 1992-93, the number of SEBs with a positive ROR were 11, there were only 6 such SEBs in 1994-95. Similarly, as against 5 SEBs with negative ROR in 1992-93, the number of such SEBs have increased to 9 in 1994-95.

There were only 3 SEBs with a ROR Return of more than 3 per cent in 1994-95. The managerial and financial inefficiencies in the state sector utilities have in turn adversely affected future capacity addition and system improvement programme. On the one hand, the SEBs do not have enough resources to finance future programmes and, on the other, their ability to raise investible funds from alternate sources in limited due to their poor financial and commerical performance.

Diagnostic studies aimed at reform and restructuring of the State power sector with a view to improving its physical and financial performance have been initiated in several States namely Haryana, Uttar Pradesh, Rajasthan, Gujarat and Andhra Pradesh. Similar studies are being considered in Kerala and Karnataka. the State of Orissa has provided the framework for reform envisaged through the enactment of a reform legislation, namely "The Orissa Reform Act, 1995" made effective from 1.495. A few other states are also considering similar steps.

The net budgetary support to the Central PSUs under the Ministry of Power as a proportion of the approved plan outlay has been declining steadily over the years. It stood at about Rs. 719.5 crore in 1996-97 and this amounted to only 10.6 per cent of total plan outlay. Owing to the decline in budgetary support, the central PSUs have to mobilise resources through internal and extra budgetary resources (IEBR). During 1995-96, the PSUs wer able to mobilise resources amounting to Rs. 3,593.8 crore as against the approved allocation of Rs. 4,326.9 crore under IEBR. Against the total plan outlay of Rs. 6,923.5 crore for the year 1995-96, the actual utilisation (Provisional) is of the order of Rs. 5,760.3 crore. During 1996-97, the IEBR component constitutes Rs. 4,565.5 crore (67 per cent) of the total approved plan outlay of Rs. 6,790.3 crore.

In view of the paucity of resources with Central/ State PSUs as well as the SEBs and the need to bridge the gap between the rapidly growing demand for the supply of electricity, there is a policy to encourage greater investment by private enterprises in the power sector. This policy, which has the objective of mobilising additional resources for capacity addition in power generation and distribution had been formulated in 1991, and is currently under implementation. The policy to invite private participation in the power sector also covers areas of transmission and distribution besides generation. The response to the policy has been expressed in putting up more than 124 power projects (requiring clearance of the Central Electricity Authority) for a total capacity of 67281 MW and involving and investment of about Rs. 2,46,472 crore. In addition, there are several projects (MOU/LOI projects costing up to Rs. 100 crore and Projects awarded through competitive bidding and costing up to Rs. 1000 crore) which are being set up by the private sector with the approval of the concerned State Government itself

In order to make the policy more attractive, the tariff notification has been amended twice to offer an assorment of incentives to investors. The Government has revised the hydro tariff guidelines to boost private investment in hydro-electric projects. To bring about private investment in the renovation, modernisation and upgradation of old power plants, the Government has finalised the policy and the guidelines have been issued. The Govenment has also taken steps to encourage captive/co-generation plants by industries. In order to encourage short gestation period projects, the Government has decided to permit setting up of power projects based on heavy fuel oils such as napha, heavy petroleum stock (HPS), low sulphur heavy stock (LSHS), heavy furnace oil (HFO), furnace oil (FO) and natural gas, wherever available, as primary fuel.

Under the current structure, the Independent Power Producers (IPPs) generally sell powers to SEBs which distribute power. Since most SEBs are financially distressed, the security package for an IPP is crucial to the success of a power project.

As an initial measure to attract private capital into the power sector, the Government of India had agreed to extend counter-guarantees to State-guarantees for the SEB's payment obligations to generating companies in respect eight fast track private power projects. This was a confidence building measure necessary for the initial batch of projects. Though these guarantees increase the comfort-levels of lenders in the initial phases, extensive use of these measures can lead to large contingent liabilities that would over-expose the concerned governments. Other options for securing the revenue stream of IPPs include Escrow Accounts, Guarantees from Multilateral Development Banks and Direct sale to high tension customers. The status of these eight fast track IPPs for which counter-guarantees have been or will be extended. Most of these projects are expecting financial and technical closure soon.

To facilitate the setting up of large sized thermal/ hydel power plants in the country, and to derive economies of scale, projects having a capacity of 1000 MW or above and supplying power to more than one stae are being considered as Mega projects. The SEBs and the State Government have been advised to introduce a more competitive element in the process of selection of selection of developers and award of projects. A notification was issued in October, 1995 enhancing concurrence of the Central Electricity Authority from Rs. 100 crore to Rs. 400 crore in the case of generating companies. The limit has been further enchanced to Rs. 1000 crore in September, 1996.

Capative power generation units in industry are used to supplement the power drawn from the grid and as a stand-by in case of power cuts. As of now, the country has an installed captive generation capacity of more than 10,000 MW. The policies relating to captive generation have also been liberalised. A 50 per cent thershold level has been prescribed for the industry's own consumption from the capative unit, and capacity in excess of this level can be sold to the grid.

In view of the widening gap between demand and supply and the huge capital cost involved in the installation of new power plants, a movement has been launched to make consumers aware of the need to save energy. Moreover, the Government is vigorously promoting energy accounting and monitoring systems. Energy audits have been carried out in a number of industrial units to identigy energy saving opportunities and eliminate wastage and to ensure that industries adopt the recommendations ofthese energy audits. Steps have been taken to improve the efficiency of domestic electrical appliances and agricultural pump sets and to promote the usage of fuel efficient engines and motors in both agricultural and transport sectors. Efforts are also being made to encourage co-generation of electricity in such industries as sugar, paper, cement, pertrochemicals and fertilisers.

The Government is working on a three-pronged strategy to overcome the existing structural constraints, technical inefficiencies and financial constraints. These include short and long-term measures to meet the power supply situation, encourage greater doses of private capital in power generation and facilitate reforms and restructuring in the state utilities. The Chief Ministers of different States met on 16th October, 1996 and 3rd December, 1996 to discuss and deliberate upon issues pertaining to the power sector. In the course of these deliberations a national consensus evolved for improving the performance of the power sector in a time bound manner and a Common Minimum National Action Plan for Power was adopted.

North-eastern Electric Power Corporation Limited (NEEPCO) was constituted in 1976 under the Companies Act to harness the power potential of the north-eastern region through planned development of power generation projects. The Corporation is responsible for operation and maintenance of the 150 mw Kopili-Hydro Electric Project which was commissioned in June/July 1988. The Corporation is presently executing the following projects: (i) Doyang Hydro-Electric Project (75 mw), Nagaland; (ii) Ranganadi Hydro electric Project (405 mw), Arunachal Pradesh; (iii) Assam Gas Based Project (291 mw), Assam; (iv) Kopali Ist stage extension Project (100 mw), Assam; and (v) Agartala Gas Turbine Project (84 mw), Tripura.

Tehri Hydro development Corporation limited (THDC) was incorporated as a joint venture public sector undertaking under the Companies Act, 1956 on 12 July 1988 for execution of Tehri Hydro Power Complex at Tehri (Garhwal) in Uttar Pradesh. The Corporation with equity participation of Government of India and Uttar Pradesh in the ratio of 75:25 (for power component of Tehri Complex) will also execute other hydro-electric projects with the consent of the state government. It has an authorised share capital of rs. 1,200 crore.

Tehri Hydro Power Complex with a generation capacity of 2400 mw comprises: (a) Tehri Dam and Hydro Powder Plant, 1000 mw (4 × 250 mw); (b) Tehri Pumped Storage Plant 1000 mw (4 × 250 mw); (c) Koteshwar Dam 400 mw (4 × 100 mw) and (d) Associated Transmission System (800 kv/400 kv) for evacuation of power. The project will generate 6,322 million units of energy per year and will provide additional irrigation facilities to 2.7 lakh hectare, besides stabilising existing irrigation facility in 6.04 lakh hectare of land.

Natpha Jhakri Power Corporation (NJPC) was incorporated on 24 May 1988 to plan, promote, organise, execute, operate and maintain hydro-electric power projects in the Satluj rover basin in Himachal Pradesh. The authorised share capital of NJPC is Rs. 1,000 crore and equity loan ratio is 1:1. Satluj river, which originates from lake Mansarover has so far been harnessed. The Nathpa Jhakri HEP is the first project taken up by the Corporation as a joint venture of Government of India and Government of Himachal Pradesh both sharing the cost of the project in the ratio of 3:1 respectively. The Nathpa Jhakri Hydro-electric project with an installed capacity of 1,500 mw is being executed by NJPC with partial assistance of 437 million US dollar from World Bank. The project is located in Kinnaur and Shimla districts of Himachal Pradesh and envisages to harness the hydro power potential in the upper reaches of river Satluj in the form of a run-of-over scheme.

Four major contracts in respect of the civil works pertaining to the Dam & Desilting Complex, the Head Race Tunnel and Surge Shaft, the Power House complex have been awarded in June - September, 1993 to three International Consortia each of whom has an Indian construction company as its partner. The work on these contracts has picked up momentum.

Damodar Valley Corporation (DVC), the first multi-purpose river valley project of the Government of India, was set up on 7 July 1948 under DVC Act (XIV of 1948) for the unified development of Damodar Valley region spread over the states of Bihar and West Bengal. DVC's objectives include flood control and irrigation, power generation and distribution, soil conservation, social and economic well-being of the people of Damodar Valley region. DVC's main projects include four dams at Maithon, Panchet, Tilaiya and Konar, four thermal power statin at Bokaro 'A', Bokaro 'B', Chandrapura and Durgapur and three hydel stations at Maithon, Panchet and Tilaiya and also one gas turbine station at Maithon.

DVC has practically become synonymous with power generation and distribution by supplying power to coal, mines, steelplants, railways and other big industries, besides state electricity boards of Bihar and West Bengal. Installed capacity of DVC in 1994-95 was 2,146 mw comprising of 1,920 mw thermal, 144 mw hydel and 82.5 mw bygas turbine. Total length of transmission lines of DVC runs over 5,000 circuit km. During the last financial year DVC generated 6,912 mw of power.

Bhakra Beas Management Board administers, maintains and operates the largest multi-purpose river valley project in the country to meet the irrigation and power needs of northern region which consitutes the granary of the nation and contributes over 90 per cent of foodgrains for the Public Distribution System. The installed capacity of power plants is 2,705 mw and the Board manages the operation of about 574 ckt km of 40 kv lines and 2,998 ckt km of 220 kv lines. The achievements during the last five years reflect complete harmony/congruence of individual and organisation goals' thereby creating synergy and a result oriented approach.

The National Power training Institute (formerly Power Engineers Training Society) was formed in 1980 as an autonomous body. The Institute is responsible for coordinating training programmes of the various state electricity boards, power stations, etc., and supplementing these with its own traiing activities. It has four regional power training institutes at Neyveli, Durgapur, Badarpur (New Delhi) and Nagpur. These institutes conduct regular induction courses, in-service refresher and short-term courses, on=job and on-plant training programmes for power engineers, operators and technicians of thermal power stations, state electricity boards, etc. A simulator installed at the training institute at Badarpur (New Delhi) Provides training to engineers and operators of 210 mw thermal units.

Central Power Research Institute (CPRI), which was set up in 1960 as a subordinate office under the erstwhile Central Water and Power Comission (Power Wing), was reorganised as a society under the Karnataka Societies

Act, 1960 w.e.f. January 1978. CPRI functions as national laboratory for applied research in the field of electric power engineering. While CPRI has its units located at Bhopal, Hyderabad, Koradi, Muradnagar and Thiruvananthhapuram, the main complex of its laboratories is at Bangalore. The Institute is an apex body for research and development in the power sector and conducts tests of electrical apparatus in accordance with national/intermational standards so as to meet fully the research and testing needs of electrical, transmission and distribution equipment. It also serves as a national testing and certification authority for transmission and distribution equipment. The Institute possesses highly sophisticated laboratories comparable to those in development countries.

Energy Management Centre (EMC) was established by the Government of India in April 1989 to act as a focal point for exchange of experience among energy institutes within India and as a centre for information, research and training activities in the energy field based on cooperation between India and the European Communities. The activities of EMC are : (i) to develop a national energy database by collecting and analysing data on energy supply, demand and infromation on prices; (ii) identify barriers for improving energy efficiency and propose appropriate incentives and other measures to overcome them.

These would include recommendations for assistance with capital investment, taxes duties and other financial incentives; (iii) to review laws and regulations that have an impact on energy consumption and propose modifications and formulate suitable policies and actions; (iv) to suggest introduction of standards, labels and setting of consumption targets; (v) to organise public infromation and promotional and promotional campaign on an on-going basis; and (vi) to organise specific promotional campaigns for the main energy consuming sectors (industry, transport, agriculture, commercial and government buildings). The Centre also provides technical assistance in the field of energy efficiency and fuel sectors; promotes energy audits enterprises and provides recommendations to improve energy efficiency and fuel substitution; and * initiates follow-up actions where needed; and organises training for energy managers and equipment operators.

The investment in Research and Development. (R & D) has increased from a paltry Rs. 20 crore in the First Five Year Plan. Presently there are 214 universities, 400 national laboratories and 1300 in-house R & D centres in the industrial sector. Several Science & Technology departments have been set up in the areas of environment, non-conventional energy resources, bio-technology, ocean development, industrial research, space, atomic energy, defence, health, agriculture and electronics.

Identification and promotion of priority areas in R & D is done by Science an Engineering Research Council (SERC) set up under the Department of Science & Technology (DST). DST supports 12 autonomous research insitutions as well, for furthering research work in several discipline. Technology Information, Forecasting and Assessment Council (TIFAC) has been set up for generating technology forecasting and technology assessment documents and enabling a technology information system that is interactive and nationally accessible.

Industrial research in several diverse fields of scientific activity is being undertaken through a network of 40 laboratories and 81 field stations set up by the Council for Scientific and Industrial Research (CSIR). In the field of bio-technology, more than 24 specialised R &

D centres have been developed for pursuing state-of-the-art research. Identical efforts for promoting new avenues of research are being undertaken in the field of ocean development as well.

The Union Budget for 1996-97 has taken various measures to promote R & D facilities. A matching one time grant has been awarded to CSIR and the Indian Council of Agricultural Research (ICAR) for modernisation of laboratories and institutes. The Technology Development and Application Fund created in 1995-96 has been proposed to be strengthened by Rs. 30 crore. A Five Year Tax Holiday under Section 80-IA of the Income Tax Act has been allowed to companies exclusively create for participation in R & D activities. The existing procedure for awarding weighted deduction under Section 35(2AA) of the Income Tax Act on sums paid for scientific research to a National Laboratory or a University or an IIT has been amended, by deleting the condition of approval by an outside body. In order to encourage R & D efforts, goods developed and patented in India and concurrently in specified countries have been exempted from levy of excise duty for a period of 3 years. The exemption procedure for customs duty on import of equipment and consumables for R & D institutions has been rationalised as well.

12

Industrial Policies

Over the years the Government of India has been adopting various measures for the liberalisation of the Industrial Policy, for streamling the licensing and foreign collaboration procedures, for reducing the number of agencies which the prospective investors have to approach to get the necessary approvals, etc., with the objective of attracting more investment and technology transfer. On the 24th July, 1991 the Government tabled before Parliament the Statement on Industrial Policy, 1991, which was followed by the issuance of a Notification by the Department of the Industrial Development to implement the Policy Statement and a series of Press Notes to set out the changes in the existing system and procedure for obtaining industrial licenses and approval of proposals for foreign and for foreign testing of indigenous raw materials and products and indigenously developed technlogies.

Industrial licensing policy

The new Industrial Licensing Policy of the Government of India has exempted form the requirement of obtaining industrial licence all industries, except those reserved for the Public Sector (Schedule I to the the Notification), those in respect of which Idustrial Licensing is compulsory (Schedule II to the Notification) and those relating to the items reserved for exclusive manufacture in the small scale sector (Schedule III to the Notification). The exemption from Industrial licensing is also subject to:

— The proposed project (except in the case of a project relating to electronics, computer software, printing industry, industry located within an area designated as 'industrial area' by a State Government before the 25th July, 1991 or the small scale or the ancillary sector) being not located with 25 kilo meters form the periphery of the standard urban area limits of a city having a population of more than one million according to the 1991 census; and

— Of the Central and the State environmental laws and regulations including local zoning and land use laws and regulations.

Units qualifying for exemption from industrial licensing in accordance with the foregoing conditions are required only to file a Memorandum in the prescribed form, before establishement of the project, with the Department of Industrial Development (Secretariat for Industrial Approvals) together with a crossed demand draft for rupees one thousand in favour of the Pay and Account Officer, Department of Industrial Development and another Memorandum in the prescribed form at the time of commencement of commercial production.

Small scale and ancillary units are required, as before, to be registered with the Director of Industries of the concerned State. Manufacturing units with an investment in plant and machinery up to Rs. 60 lakhs, ancillary units with an investment in plant and machinery up to Rs. 75 lakhs and units which are willing to undertake an export obligation to the extend of 30 per cent of their annual production by the third year with an investment up to Rs. 75 lakhs are eligible for small scale registration.

Trade policy

Side by side with the announcement of New Industrial Policy for Promoting Small Tiny and Village Enterprises, the Government have also announced major reforms in the Trade Policy. The main objective of the trade policy have been to progressively reduce the system of administrative controls and lilcences and to link import except in the case of essential items. The major reforms in the Trade Policy are given below:

Introduction of eximscrip system

Exports were in the past allowed replenishment to provide for essential inputs required for the manufacture of products exported. To allow flexibility to enable diversification of export products and also as an incentive for exports, the REP licenses so issued, were allowed to be freely sold.

The entitlement for REP licenses also varied from item to item. In view of the flexibility of the REP Licenses Government realise that to treat it as licence is an misnomer, under the new policy the REP licences have been replaced by a new instrument named 'Eximscrips'. Eximscrips will be issued on the basis of FOB value of exports or Net FOreign Exchange (NFE) earnings from exports as indicated below. The main features of the new systems are:

(i) The basic rate at which Eximscripts will be issued against exports will be 30% of FOB value. Exports to hard currency areas will be eligible for Eximscrips valid for hard currency imports while exports to rupee payment areas will be issued Eximscrips valid for imports from these areas only. However, as a measure of transition, exports to rupee payment areas may continue to avail of REP licences valid for hard currency imports at the rate prevailing prior to

4th July, 1991. This transition facility will be available only for exports effected upto 31st December 1991.

(ii) Products such as gems and jewellery, handcrafts, newspapers, journals and periodicals and cinematographic films, which enjoyed higher rated of REP will receive Eximscrips at the same rates as before.

(iii) The Basis rate of 30% is inadequate for exports of certain products such as value-added agricultural projects, electronics, bulk drugs and marine products, formulations and certain categories of advanced engineering goods. These products will be eligible for an additional Eximscrips entitlement of 10 percentage points, taking the total Eximscrips rate to 40% of FOB value.

For exports made on the basis of duty free imports obtained against Advance Licences, Eximscrips will be available at the general rate of 30% but this will be applied to the net foreign exchange earnings. On the same principle. Eximscrips at 30% of NFE will also be available for all EOU and EPZ units.

(iv) The 30% of NFE rate of Eximscrips is also applicable to service exports, including software exports which is a thrust area. The definition of services covered under this category is being ratinallized and extended to include other services such as services of architects, textile designers, artists, management consultants, lawyers etc. The benefit will be available to services exported by resident Indians for which remittances are made to India. The details are being notified separately.

Eximscrips issued to exporters will be tradeable and can be used to import any item in the limited permissible list

(Appendix-3), the non-sensitive canalised list (Appendix-5A) and for all OGL, items for actual users (Appendix-6, List 8, Part I and List 10). Eximscrips earned by exporters on their own exports can also be used to import non-OGL capital goods other than those on the restricted list (Appendix-1A). All REP licences issued against exports prior to 4th July, 1991 will continue to be valid for the life of the licence and will have the same import entitlement as the new Eximscrips. Additional licences issued to export houses/trading houses, which were earlier valid for a more limited range of imports, will also be valid for the same range of imports as Eximscrips.

With the introduction of Eximscrips, the system of issuing supplementary licences of raw material, components and spares listed in Appendix-3 will be discontinued except for small scale industries and for manufacturers of specified life saving drugs and equipment. In future, all import requirements of these items (with the exceptions indicated above) will be made through Eximscrips, Similarly items in Appoendix-4 and Appendix-9, which were earlier importable against supplementary licences, will henceforth be importable only against Eximscrips. Import of items appearing in Appendix-2 Part B (list of Restricted Items) and Appendix-8 (List of Scientific and Measuring Instruments Restricted for Import) of the Import-Export Policy 1990-93 will continue to require licences. Such licences as well as licences required for small scale industries and manufactures of life saving drugs/equipment will be called Special Licences as these will be limited and include special cases.

As a measure of import compression and to strengthen the linkage between import capability and exports, two further changes have been made. The category of unlisted OGL has been abolished and these items have been shifted to Appendix-3. They are now importable only against Eximscrips (except for SSI and manufacturers of life saving drugs and equipment). In the case of units subject to the Phased Manufacturing Programme (PMP), many of which benefit from concessional duty on their imports of OGL items, all such items will henceforth be importable only against Eximscrips.

Eximscrips will be issued only after export proceeds have been realised. The procedure for issue of Eximscrips has been streamlined and Government will ensure that Eximscrips are issued within 48 hours of the receipt of the application accompanied by single document, namely, the bank certificate for the realisation of export proceeds.

Advance licences

The system of advance licences is designed to provide exporters with duty free access to the inputs they need to produce competitively for world markets. This is an important instrument of trade policy especially in our situation where tariff levels are still high. The Government has taken the following steps to strengthen the system of Advance Licences as an instrument of export promotion:

(i) The procedures for considering Advance Licence applications have been simplified to ensure that advance licences will be issued within 15 days of application in all cases where input-output norms have been fixed. Where norms have not been fixed, the licence will be issued within 45 days.

(ii) The number of documents accompanying an Advance licence application has been reduced from 9 to 3 where norms are prescribed and to 4 where they are not prescribed.

(iii) Ar present norms have been prescribed for 540 items. This will be increased to over 1000 items by 31st October, 1991 and more items will be covered thereafter.

(iv) Substantial Manufacturing Activity as a necessary condition under the Advance Licence Scheme will no longer be applicable for exports to the general currency area. However, the value addition norms will remain in force. A large number of exporters will benefit under this scheme.

(v) A new Scheme of Transferable Advance Licence has been introduced for GCA exports in selected thrust areas, namely textiles, leather goods and engineering industries. Under this scheme exporters can undertake exports based on duty paid inputs obtained from the market and subsequently obtain advance licences for replenishment of these inputs by duty free imports. These advance licences will be freely transferable. The coverage of the scheme will be extended on merits.

(vi) Advance licence will specify values in free foreign exchange both for the purpose of import and export. The currencies in which such values are denominated will be limited to those notified for this purpose by the RBI.

(vii) The Existing procedure for obtaining Bank Guarantee (BG) and Legal Undertaking (LUT) from different categories of exporters in being streamlined and liberalised as follows:

(a) Export/Trading/Star Trading House and Public Sector Undertakings will have the facility of obtaining advance licence against LUT only without any monetary limit.

(b) All manufacturing units having an annual turnover of at least Rs. 5 crores (including both domestic and exports turnover) during the previous 3 year would also be able to avail of the LUT facility up to a value limit of 50% of their annual production.

(c) A new unit without any production or export performance to its credit would also be allowed LUT facility provided it is promoted by an existing company with an annual production of Rs. 5 crores for more than three years. In such a case, both the new company and the promoting company would have to provide LUT.

(d) Bank guarantee and/or LUT obligation will be concurrent to the fulfilment of export obligation.

(viii) Exporters would be allowed to dispose of the materials imported against advance licences by way of replenishment without seeking prior permission of the licensing authority in cases where no MODVAT facility has been availed of on the domestic material used in exports.

(ix) Adjustment needed on account of fluctuation of prices of imported individual items would be permitted within the overall CIF value of advance licence.

(x) The power of revalidation which presently vests in the Licencing Committee at the Headquarters has been delegated to the Licensing Authorities.

(xi) In case where applications for an advance licence are turned down, the exporter will be permitted to convert to the Duty Drawback regime by the Collectors of Customs so that shipments made in advance can be imported on payment of duty subsequent claims of duty drawback.

(xii) Exporters can obtain advance release orders for domestic supply against advance licences under which the domestic supplier gets the benefit of deemed exports. Henceforth, release orders will be issued across the counter without requiring the name of the domestic supplier, which could be given later.

The adoption of these procedures would reduce discretionary controls and delays and afford much greater freedom to exporters in procuring essential duty free raw materials to maintain their competitiveness in the would market thereby promoting exports from the country.

Export processing zones and 100% EOUs

The export Processing Zone scheme and the 100% EOU scheme were introduced to provide for duty-free enclaves, which would enable entrepreneurs to concentrate on production exclusively for export. However, with increasing liberalisation in the DTA, the duty advantages enjoyed by EPZs/EOUs have become less important. While the procedures of Customs Bonding are very onerous. The schemes have not therefore taken off as expected and they have also not attracted foreign investment aimed at tapping export markets to the extent that was expected. The working of these schemes has been reviewed and the following changes made:

(i) All EOUs/EPZ unit will be eligible for Eximscrips at the basic rate of 30% applied to net foreign exchange earning.

(ii) The duty applicable on DTA sales from EOUs/EPZ units is being reduced to 50% of the normal customs subject to the duty payable not being less than the excise duty on the same product. The extent of DTA sales allowed will be accordance with their entitlement. DTA sales will be permitted in the ratio of 25:75 in relation to export sales in case of units while use of indigenous raw material is more than 30% of production. In all other cases the ratio of permissible DTA sales to export sales will be 15:85. The procedures for clearing goods from the EOU/EPZ units for DTA sales are also being streamlined.

(iii) In order to encourage exporters to set up EOUs or EPX units the net foreign exchange earned by EOUs or EPZ units can be clubbed with the earnings of their parent/associated companies in the DTA for the purpose of according Export House. Trading House of Star Trading House status for the latter.

(iv) The IPRS scheme for supply of steel to exporters will also be extended to EOUs and EPZ units. The Development Commissioners are being empowered to issue "payment authorities" in lieu of JCCI & Es.

Under the New Industrial Policy, most industries do not require an industrial licence except for a defined list. With a view to bringing about comparable streamlining in the procedure for EOU/EPZ approvals, a systems of automatic approvals is being established for all proposals which fall within certain parameters. Capital goods imports will be allowed under the automatic approvals procedure if they are fully covered by foreign equity or if they do not exceed 50% of the value of plant and equipment subject to a ceiling of Rs 3 crores. All proposals within the automatic approval parameters will be cleared within two weeks. All other proposals will be submitted to the Board of Approvals for consideration and decisions including issue of licences will be taken within 45 days.

A large number of issues relating to the operation of EOUs/EPZ units required centralized clearance in the

Ministries of Commerce and Industry. Powers are being delegated to the Development Commissioners so that these approvals can be given on a decentralised basis. The specific approval of the Development Commissioner would not be required in cases of broad banding by EPZ units, where value addition is being maintained. The unit concerned would need only to provide relevant information to the Development Commissioner.

The following specific concessions to EOUs/EPZ units have also been extended:

(i) Allowing wntry of imported raw material on "Provisional Assessment" basis, to expedite customs clearance.

(ii) Permitting units under the EPZ and EOU schemes to supply/transfer finished goods among themselves.

(iii) Replacement of multiple bond by a single bond, for obtaining import clearance.

(iv) Increasing the list of items under the "Special Imprest Licence Scheme" on selective basis.

(vi) Clarifying that containers stuffed in EPZ and EOUs are not to be reinspected at other points, as long as seals are intact.

Government have also decided to allow private parties to establish bonded warehouses within EPZs for stocking and sale of duty free raw materials, components, consumables and spares to EPZ units and EOUs. This will cut down delay in obtaining supplies of duty free materials which are in constant and regular demand by exporters. The details of this scheme will be notified shortly.

Other steps announced in the new Trade Policy have been the simplification of procedures for import of capital goods, decanalisation of number of items which were previously canalised, permission to allow established exporters to open foreign currency accounts in approved banks, raise external credits, pay for export related imports from such accounts and credit export proceeds to such accounts, its decision to re-designate the office of the Chief Controller of Import and Exports as Directorate General of International Trade with the principal function being to promote of exports, and facilitation of imports to promote export trade.

Reduction in import licence

The policy changes now being implemented imply substantial reduction in the extent of licensing and in the number of types of licences. Supplementary licences for import of items in Appendixes-3 (except for SSI and manufacturers of life saving drugs and equipment), 4 and 9 of the Import-Export Policy 1990-93 have been abolished. Additional licences which were issued as an incentive to Export Houses and Trading Houses will stand abolished with effect from 1st April, 1992 and the incentive will take the form of an additional Eximscrip entitlement.

To achieve optimal import containment in the context of the present Balance of Payments situation, several steps have been taken. One of these is the shift of many items which are on OGL to the limited permissible list.

With these changes, the policy for import of raw materials components and other inputs needed for production has been simplified. Most raw materials and other inputs (except for those on the Restricted List) can be freely imported either against Eximscrips or on OGL. Some raw materials continue to be canalised but in more of these cases requirements beyond those provided by the canalising agencies can be met through Eximscrips.It is the policy of the Government to move to a situation where imports of essential raw materials and components needed for industrial production are regulated through appropriate tariffs. However, in view of the Balance of Payments position which necessitates continued import containment, this cannot be done immediately. Many items must therefore remain on the limited permissible list, with imports permitted only against Eximscrips.

The medium term objective of the Government is to progressively eliminate licensing and quantitative restrictions on capital goods and raw materials/ components so that all these items can be placed on OGL save for a small carefully defined negative list. This shift is proposed to be achieved over a 3 to 5 year period. The Government will appoint a High Level Committee to work out the modalities of achieving this transition keeping in mind the Balance of Payments position and the need to rationalise the reduce tariffs progressively to provide Indian Industry with an appropriate environment to develop international competitiveness.

International trade and India

1. The important place commanded by India in world trade in coffee, tea, leather and spices on a historical basis has continued in recent years as wll. In 1994, India accounted for 2.4 per cent, 13.6 per cent, 2.5 per cent and 9.1 per cent of world trade in coffee and coffee substitues, tea and mate, leather, and spices, respectively. Furthermore, there has been a significant progress in export diversification, and India has emerged as an important exporter of iron ore and concentrates, and pearis, precious and semi-precious stones. In 1994, India accounted for 6 per cent or world exports of iron ore and concentrates

and 10.9 per cent of world exports of pearls, precious and semi precious stones (Source: 1994 United Nations International Trade Statistics Year Book, 1995).

2. During 1950, India accounted for about 1.8 per cent (1.85 per cent of exports and 1.71 per cent of imports) of world trade. After gradually declining to 0.57 per cent by 1980, India's share improved marginally to 0.63 per cent by 1985. The reason for improvement in the share was that while world trade declined in the period 1980-85, India's trade continued to grow. However it came down again to 0.53 per cent by 1991. The first half of the nineties witnessed a sharp increase in India's exports and imports have grown in dollar terms annually by 12.4 per cent and 9.4 per cent, respectively. The corresponding growth rates of world trade was about 5.7 per cent. The secular decline in India's share in world trade has been arrested and reversed, and the years ahead are likely to see a continuation of this increasing trend.

3. The trade policy components of the reform process undertaken since July 1991 have been motivated by a full recognition of the important role that trade can play in promoting growth. The utilisation of the expanded scope for specialising in areas of comparative advantage is manifest in the improved growth performance of the economy. Furthermore, while exports have vigorously responded to the removal of the anti-export bias of a protectionist environment, domestic industry appears to have been stimulated by the expended availability of imported inputs and capital goods as well as the challenge of competing in the international market place. The positive response of Indian industry to

liberalisation is amply demonstrated by the capital goods sector. The tariff on capital goods was as high as 85 per cent in the pre-reforms period. This has been reduced to about 25 per cent covering about 80 per cent of capital goods in 1995-96. The capital goods industry which witnessed a negative growth of 12.8 per cent in 1991-92, registered an average growth of about 23 per cent during 1994-96.

4. The terms of trade, which measure the terms of exchange between a unit of exports and a unit of imports, have been improving in the post-reform period. Two common ways of measuring the terms of trade are the net terms of trade (NTT) and the income terms of trade (ITT). A time series indicating all parameters of terms of trade (TOT) for India since 1969-70 with the base of 1978-79 = 100 Indicates that there have been wide fluctuations in the TOT. The NIT (1978-79=100), which is an index of export prices divided by an index of import prices, improved from 109.3 in 1990-91 to 152.4 in 1994-95. It is

5. It may be mentioned that India s purchasing power of exports as reflected thorough ITT has been improving continuously since 1985- 86. The value index of exports at 484 stands much higher than that of imports at 351 and hence, in terms of value, india has gained.But in terms of volume, the index of exports has been much less at 384 in comparison to that of imports at 515. This means that the volume of imports is increassing faster, though India is getting a better price for her exports.

6. Compared to the experience of other developing countries, the improvement in the terms of trade for India has been very impressive.

7. Developing economies, with exports dominated by primary products, lost out to developed economies. Relavtive abundance of supply of primary products as well as the superior bargaining strength of developed countries have often ben adduced as two major reasons for the deterioration in the terms of trace. Gains in the terms of trade for India in the comparable period perhaps reflects her diversified export base as well as the relatively low international prices of oil in the relevant period.

India is committed to further liberalisation of its import regime, notwithstanding the dismantling of licensing controls over a wide area. At the same time, there are concerns whether developed nations of the world are implementing in letter and spirit their part of the obligations under the Uruguay Round Agreements. Many contries are resorting to protectinist devices in the guise of environmental hazards and exploitation of labour such as child labour. The obligations of providing access to imports of developing countries, especially textiles and garments, are being circumvented under one pretext or the other, even under the back-loaded integration of Textiles and Clothing into the World Trading System. Such restrictions are designed to keep out cheaper imports.

By virtue of the radical shift from a highly-regulated to an outward-oriented economy, India has attracted immense interest abroad, at both Governmental and private investor levels. India is one of the largest emerging markets, second only to China's, and the country has been experiencing inflows of foreign portfolio and direct investments—thought not as large as in China and a few other countries—which were unthinkable in the world of even 1980s. Economic strength has become the principal determinant of a nation's standing in the international community, and even the most powerful country, the United States of America, looks for market opportunities all over, more especially in the dynamic Asia-Pacific region, as the best shield of security.

With the end of the Cold War, the East-West barriers have broken down. The rapid spread of liberalisation and globalisation is a historic development which has blurred both East-West and North-South divisions. Developing countries have been compelled to adapt themselves to conditions of global interdependence although in the process they run grave risks in the medium-term and rare not assured of international safety nets.

In the rapidly changing world environment, each developing country must certainly concentrate on building its inherent strength and developing areas of comparative advantage and forge alliances with neighbours and, where promising, enter regional blocs which offer greater opportunities of trade and other exchanges to enhance national arena, disadvantaged nations must make common cause and unite to advance their pressing needs more effectively than what has been witnessed over the last fifty years in the post-decolonisation era. This is the only way of securing a post-cold war order which is just and equitable.

India has a long way to go before it could emerge as a strong global player, as currently it occupies the 32nd place as a leading exporter of merchandise, well below several countries in East and South-East Asia. It has to make up for the time lost in its inward-looking route to development which left the cuntry far behind in the international league, despite building a strong industrial base and possessing highly technical manpower, the third largest in the world. Indian planning did not take sufficient note of the gathering pace of global intergration with the frowth of merchandise trade exceeding the growth of output in virtually every year of the post-war period.

In recent years, India has begun to look East, is now a full dialogue partner in ASEAN (the 7-member Association of South East Nations) and excepts to find a place in the Asia Pacific Economic Forum (APEC) by 1999. These should promote greater intra-Asian trade and investment flows even as India strives to gain an increasing share of exports into developed economies of the West such as the European Union and North America. Trade with Russia and Eastern Europe as well as Central Asian States holds prospects of considerable expansion over present levels and a more promising development is the initiative taken by 14 states of the Indian Ocean Rim for an economic cooperation grouping with a Charter expected to be signed in March 1997

The bilateral and pluralistic approaches cannot, and should not, in any way dilute India's firm commitment to multilaterialism which is the best safeguard against domination of the global economy by a few powerful nations. India's immediate responsibility is to solidify South Asian cooperation through SAPTA and ensure its early graduation to becomes SAFTA (South Asian Free Trade Area) to make it a region of good neighbourliness less prone to conflilcts than at present. With 16 per cent of the world's population, India's weight in the international economy remains negligible, and the building up of internal strength with determination through higher saving, and investments and greater efficiency in the use of resources is a pre-requisite for the country to claim its due share in the global market-place.

The kingpin of India's foreign policy has broadly been dictated by a principle of equidistance form the Superpower rivalry until the dissolution of the Soviet

Union. In any assessment of India's role to ensure global peace, non-aligned movement played an important part. Although the movement never functioned on any bloc concept, it became the voice of vast multitudes of people spanning four continents belonging to the developing world.

The non-aligned movement was launched in Belgrade in 1961. Eminent statesmen who pioneered the movement were Prime Minister Jawaharlal Nehru, President Tito of Yugoslavia and President Gamel Nasser of Egypt. The movement which had only a handful of members initially later grew into a formidable number. The current chairmanship of Colombia, once believed to be an Americanally in Latin America, is a clear proof that the movement's appeal was spreading to South America, usually considered as "backyard" of US sphere of influence.

The disappearance of the Soviet Union brought an end to Superpower rivalry. It had its effect on the non-aligned movement. Except the coordinating bureau of non-aligned countries at the United Nations, the movement never though it appropriate to have a headquarters. This never gave rise to absence of cohesion in the movement's functioning. In contrast, the Organisation of Africa Unity (OAU) has its headquarters in Addis Ababa, while the Arab League is located in Caero.

Non-aligned movement could have been more powerful as a political force at international level had China preferred to join it. Mao Zedong divided the world into "three worlds" according to the level of economic development. Surely, China fitted in with the concept of "third world", embracing the developing countries. But at no point of time since 1961China a expressed the desire to be part of non-aligned movement, although China rightly belongs to the developing world. India's third conribution to world peace came from its unremitting support to the anti-apartheid movement in South Africa and its support to decolonisation. New Delhi never gave up the cause of the black South Africans and the Black Africans in the rest of the continent, despite repression on their movement and denial of basic human rights by the colonising powers. One after the other, the French, Portuguese and Dutch colonisers left territories ruled by them. But South Africans were yet to see the light at the end of the tunnel.

The paths to peace and freedom and equal rights were strewn with thorns and hurdles were placed at all steps. the White rule became a blot on the world conscience. Denial to right to live brought an upsurge among the Black South Africans. In their struggle, they found India and the Indians settled there as a great source of inspiration. It was not because Mahatma Gandhi's association with South Africa in the initial years of his political life that made India so receptive to the aspirations of the Black South Africans.

Perhaps in the South African freedom movement and struggle for equality was seen the same psyche of the Indian people who suffered humiliation, imprisonment and torture in India during the long independence struggle. Indians felt genuinely for the Black South Africans. So did the goverment.

In less than a decade's existence as an independent nation, India brought before the world a new concept of governance based on the principle of "Panchsheel". It was but natural for a country that has a long tradition of tolerance. India with numerous languages and multiplicity of religion itself symbolises co-existence. Mutual respect for each other, irrespective of differences, demonstrates Indian ethos.

It is in this context, the Bandung conference in April 1955 that adopted "Panchsheel" created a new concept for the world already handed over to violence and turmoil. The Bandung conference had five proponents: India, Indonesia, Burma, Sri Lanka and Pakistan. The Bandung conference was preceded by the bombing of the Air India plane carrying delegates and journalists over South China sea. Evidently, forces that wanted the settlement of disputes through terrorism asserted their right to show their way of solving issue and problems.

Foreign economic relations

Government of India continued to give special and focussed attention to economic diplomacy at the bilateral, regional and multilateral levels. Government's efforts is to expand existing opportunities and create new ones for trade, investment and technological cooperation with the industrialised, newly industrialising and developing countries.

India's engagement in economic cooperation among a trans-regional group of developing countries in Asia, Latin America and Africa assumed special significance. The 4th Summit of the G-15 was held in New Delhi from 28 to 30 March 1994. It was decided to broaden the scope of intra G-15 cooperation through the establishment of a Committee of Trade, Investment and Technology to work towards evolution of trans-regional arangements for liberalisation, facilitation and promotion of trade, investment and technology transfer.

The Summit decided to harness the information and communication revolution to promote better understanding and knowledge of capabilities, potential and experiences of G-15 countries among each other and extend full support through appropriate projects for expanding cooperation in setting up of small scale industreis.

At the 30th Anniversary commemoration meeting of the Group of 77 held in New York in July 1994, India reaffirmed the historical validity of the concept, purpose and endeavours of the Group of 77. By inserting a development dimension and consensus in international institutions and policies, the G-77 had acted as a development conscience of the world and recorded some gains in this respect.

Progress has been made in establishment on an ASEAN-India Trade and Investment Information and Promotion Centre, collaboration and joint ventures in India, ASEAN and third countries; cooperation in tourist destination, development and exchange of information and technology.

In July 1994 India gave a detailed presentation to OECD on economic reforms inititated by India, which was followed by a visit by the President of the OECD Development Centre to India. A break-through in closer association with the OECD was achieved in December 1994 when the OECD Council approved inclussion of India along with Indonesia and China in their OECD Policy Dialogue framework with Dynamic New Major Economies (DNMEs). India continued to further fine tune, adapt and expand her ECDC and TCDC programmes under the ITEC programme and the SCAAP for the benefit of developing countries mainly in Africa, Latin America, Caribbean and South East Asia. During 1994-95, 875 slots have been allocated for training of foreign nominees in Indian civilian institutions and 65 regular courses are being held in 30 prominent institutions in banking, small scale industries, finance, tool research, etc. India also offered military training to nominees from friendly foreign countreis.

Under the ITEC programme, projects are executed in partner countries, among other things, such projects serve as demonstration models highlighting India's technology and potential in specific areas. Under execution are Vocational Training Centres in Vietnam and Mongolia, Solar Photovoltaic Plants in Oman and Cuba, a Remote Sensing Centre in Mauritius and a Mobile Eye Clinic in Ghana. Execution of feasibility studies/extension of consultancy services in partner countries are also undertaken under ITEC.

The SCAAP programme is aimed at providing technical assistance by India to 15 African counries which are ex-colonies of UK. In 1994-95, a total of 475 slots were allocated to nominees from Ghana, Nigeria, Mauritius, Tanzania and Zambia. A new dimension was attempted to be given to Indian's policy of South-South Cooperation through the Special volunteers Programme (SVP). The SVP envisages the sending of special volunteers to developing countries in Africa and Asia to assist them in their development programmes. During 1994-95, disaster relief assistance has been/is being extended to Armenia, Tanzania, Mozambique, Afghanistan, Uzbekistan, Rawanda, Somalia, Madagascar, Djibouti, Mauritius, etc. Such humanitarian gestures strike a positive chord amongst the people of these countries and create goodwill for India.

Trade and investment promotion

One of the most important forces current developments today is the emergence of a truly global economy. India's economic reforms programme reflects her determination to build an economy that is internationally competitive and integrated into the global economy.

Investment promotion seminars have been organised in Japan, Germany, singapore, Thailand, Australia,l Italy and USA, wide publicity was given to international fairs organised in India like IITF'94, International Seminar on

Mineral and Mineral-based industries in ESCAP Region'94, MANTECH'95, IETF'95, AGROEXPO'95, Gifts and Handicrafts Fair'95 and 22nd World Marketing and Management congress'95. Special efforts were made to reach out to business journalists in foreign countries by arranging their visits to India in order to enable them to see first hand the changes in the business environment. Prime Minister's visits to the UK, Russia, USA, Vietnam and Singapore, as well as visits by Ministers and prominent economic personalities were utilised to highlight the opportunities for economic collaborations and business tie-ups with India. In the course of the Prime Minister's visit to Singapore in September 1994, 12 agreements were signed between Indian and Singaporean companies in diverse fields.

Various investment promotion seminars were also organised in India.Prominenet among these were INVESTMART organised in April 1994 by Ministry of Industry in collaboration with UNIDO. The entire forum was focussed on promoting 250 specific projects identified in specific sectors by Ministry of Industry. France, Italy, UK, USA and Singapore participated. About 70 Letters of Intent for identified projects were signed between Indian entrepreneurs and foreign collaborators.

Trade scenario in post-independence era

By virtue of the radical shift from a highly-regulated to an outward-oriented economy, India has generated immense interest abroad, but it has a long way to go before emerging as a strong global player, opines the author. India's development strategy launched in the 1950s, soon after Independence, aimed mainly at strengthening the industrial base of the country, especially in basic goods and heavy machine-building, and adopted the import-substituation model to achieve self-reliance. Rxports were not viewed as an integral part of overall economic development, and such imports as became unavoidable were financed by drawing down foreign exchange reserves that had accrued to India at the time of Independence, in the form of sterling balances held in its favour for goods and services provided by this country during the Second World War.

Export pessimism dominated the mood of the early planners as it was rightly assumed then that until India's manufactures began to be diversified, there was little possibility of exporting manufactures while primary products and traditional manufactured goods faced poor demand prospects in the world market. It was during the later half of the fifties, when the Second Five Year Plan was under way with its emphasis on heavy industry, largely in the public sector, that it began to be realised that India needed to export to be able to finance at least part of the maintenance and developmental imports.

The foreign exchange crisis that was looming by mid-1957 reinforced the importance of export growth as part of planned development. The pessimistic view about the potential for export earnings gave way to a more positive approach in the Third Plan (1961-66) with the introduction of export promotion measures without deflecting from the thrust of import subsitution and industrialisation. It was clear by mid-estimated the import content of the inward-looking path of development opted by India. Pressures on balance of pyaments had already brought into existence the Aid-India-Consortium comprising the World Bank and developed countries interested in providing assistance to India. Renewed emphasis on exports was laid in the Fourth Plan (1969-74) which envisaged porogressive elimination of dependence on foreign aid while the Fifth Plan (1974-79) identified certain sectors such as engineering goods, garments, leather manufacture and marine products for achieving increases in exports.

Thus, as agianst virtual stagnation in the 1950s, export performance improved to an average growth of 3 to 4 per cent in the 1960s, and was more impressive in 1970s with an average growth of 6.3 per cent in volume and 15.9 per cent in value terms.

But in the three decades, India's share in world exports had declined throughout from about 2 per cent in 1950 to 0.65 per cent in 1970 and dropped further to 0.42 per cent in 1980. This was the period when there was impressive grow thin world trade and the opportunities were seize by many smaller Asian developing countries as well as the industrialising economies in Latin America to great advantage.

Paradoxically, even as india's export growth was being maintained or marginaly improved upon, her share of world exports was declining. Over the three decades ending the Seventies, the share of exports in Gross Domestic Product (GDP) ranged from 4 to 6 per cent. In a continental economy of India's size, the role of external sector in the development process was under-played so much that it took a successions of droughts, oil price shocks and balance of payments difficulties in the first two and a half decades of planning before the country could begin to see import substitution and export promotion as two sides of the same coin. But heavy reliance on quantitative restrictions on trade through import and export controls and detailed industrial licensing kept India a closed economy. Industrial Policy and Trade Policy of the Government of India

Foreign investment policy

The new industrial policy of the Government of India has

announced major liberalisation for attracting foreign investment in respect of a list of high priority industries (Annexure III to the Statement of Industrial Policy, 1991). Foreign equity investment up to 51 per cent will be allowed subject only to the condition that:

— The requirement of imported capital goods should be covered by the foreign equity;

— Remittance of dividends should be covered by earnings of the company from export of items in Annexure III to the Statement of Industrial Policy, 1991. The amount of dividend payment may be converted by export earnings of such items recorded in Years prior to the payment of dividend or in the year of payment of dividend. This will be monitored by the Reserve Bank of India. However, such balancing will not be required beyond a period of seven years from commencement of production.

In all such cases the Reserve Bank of India has been authorised to issue automatic approvals of foreign investment and also grant exemption from the operation of the relevant sections of the Foreign Exchange Regulations Act, 1973.

Ushering in an era of scripless trading

The Primary issuance of securities has a long history in India. The Indian bond market, measured by the estimated value of bonds outstanding, is next only to the Japanese and the Korean bond market in Asia. By January 31, 1995, the outstanding value of the Indian securities market was estimated to have reached Rs.3000 billion, almost 3.5 times its size in 1986. The size is deceptive as, despite attractive yields, secondary market trading has remained poor with virtually no quotation even in respect of listed securities. The estimated outstanding amount accounts for about 42% of GDP, as at the end of January 1995. Partial deregulation of interest rates in the early nineties and increasing emphasis on monetary policy in stabilization are the first major steps towards the emergence of an active debt market, with government securities spearheading the process. With the issuance of government securities at market determined coupon rates and the use of innnovative products, it has become possible, for the first time, for other issuers to offer debt products priced off the yield on government securities.

The process of financial sector reforms initiated in 1991, is far from complete. The Growth of the Indian Capital Market since Independence has been phenomenal. The number of stock exchanges increased from 7 in 1947 to 23 in 1994. Likewise the number of listed companies on stock exchanges grew from 1125 in 1946 to 7811 at the end of 994. Similarly, the quantum of listed capital registered a growth of about 565 times from Rs.270 crore in 1946 to Rs.152,322 crore at the end of March, 1994.

The basic objective of financial sector reforms is to promote a diversified, efficient and competitive financial system by a policy shift from detailed regulation and controls to one based on market forces. Alongwith dismantling administrative regulation, the goal is establishment of a system of prudential regulation, supported by a mechanism for reporting, monitoring and supervision of the compliance.

Another major plan of reform is injection of new competition into a hitherto virtually government owned financial system. For the first time in many years, six new banking licences have been granted to the private sector all of which have been implemented. The new banks are permitted to have financial joint ventures with fgoreign baks, particularly for accessing modern systems and technology. There has been a mushrooming of Non-Banming Finance Companies (NBFCs), some of whom have already built up a large net-work. Several well known investment banks have established a presence in India. Since April 1993, nearly 300 Foreign Institutional Inestors (FIIs) have been registered with the regulatory authority and quite a few are active investors in the domestic capital market which has been opened up to foreign portfolio investment in a limited way. Several new mutual funds have been set up by the private sector including some by global fund managers. The most spectacular growth has been registered when we compare the share of market capitalization to gross domestic products (GDP) which was 12.9% in 1946, while in 1991-92 it was 57.2% and further increased to 68.8% during 1993-984.

Growth & development of Indian consultancy

The Indian consultancy scenario is a rich blend of both "self-developed" technology on one hand and "acquired" know-how on the other. When the country emerged into freedom in 1947 the Indian Economy was at a low ebb with impoverished resources, processes and infrastructure designed to meet vested requirements and an environment wherein the wherewithal for nurturing and training technical and managerial talent was hardly there. The country soon took stock of the situation. National priorities were identified and a well conceived policy of "planned development" was adopted. Economic re-generation & growth forced an important segment in these planning programmes with socio-economic factors, like medicare, education, technical training, employment etc. appropriately dovetailed. It was recognised that for all these programmes or activities it was essential to nurture, encourage and develop an effective cadre of professionals, both technical and managerial. The concept of consultancy was thus ushered in and gathered strength gradually.

Self-reliance

In the course of these four score and more years-in an environment of growth and development-the Indian consultant has been sufficiently exposed not only to the technological development and consultancy practices in other countries but also is a part of the indigenous consultancy culture that has evolved as an achievement towards the national objective of self-reliance. India's commitment to self-reliance in engineering skills has ensured a fairly good growth of the consultancy sector. As a part of the overall strategy for industrial development, the utilisation of indigenous design and engineering inputs is one of the key factors. The sixties and seventies witnessed the emergence of several consultancy organisations, with specialisation in various sectors of industry. Some of these were set up in collaboration with foreign organisations while many others were set up totally with local expertise.

CDC/FIEO survey

According to a survey recently conducted by the Consultancy Development Centre (CDC) and the Federation of Indian Export Organisations (FIEO), Both non-profit institutions set up by the Government of India to service Indian Consultancy-there are more then 1400 consultancy organisations and individual consultants (both management and technical) rendering services in various aspects of industrial and non-industrial sectors of the economy.

Trend of growth

The trend of growth of consultancy during the periods 1940-1988 is shown in the Table below:

Growth Trend of Indian Consultancy

Period	Annual Growth %
1940 – 60	5
1961 – 80	43
1981 – 88	52

Growth indicators

During the course of the last 5 years the number of consultancy firms in the country has country has increased from 700 to 1400; the consultancy turnover from Rs. 500 to Rs. 1000 crores; employment in the consultancy profession from 40,000 to 80,000 and exports of consultancy services from Rs. 50 to Rs. 120 crores.

Nascent stage

In spite of this growth, and keeping in mind that the consultancy culture has assumed some dimensions in India's national economic infrastructure only recently, Indian consultancy, in spite of its achievements, is yet in its nascent stage.

The three decades of continues growth have brought maturity to the movement of entrepreneurship development in India. Till the beginning of the 1960s, entrepreneurship remained a topic of academic and philosophical discussion by economist, sociologist and psychologist. The attempt was to accurately define and describe entrepreneurship, its nature and functions. Such description were markedly influenced by respective academic disciplines.

Although most of these descriptions were partly true, yet none of them had the quality of describing entrepreneurship as a whole. Towards the end of the 60s, two very significant contributions were made in the field of entrepreneurship. These were:

(i) Establishment of positive linkages between entrepreneurship and economic prosperity. 1 and

(ii) Emergence of strong hypothese that entrepreneurship can be developed through planned efforts. 2

The former helped acceptance of entrepreneurship development for achieving economic prosperity and the later facilitated experimentation with various strategies for developing entrepreneurship.

In 70's varieties of strategies and models of developing entrepreneurship were developed, repeated and replicated. As a result entrepreneurship was identified as important vehicle of industrial development which is evident by the emergence of about 1.7 million SSI enterprises creating jobs for more than 10 million workers in the sector. During 80's the structure and functions needed for promoting entrepreneurship become more or less clear and entrepreneurship attained the status of a movement. At national level during 1982-83 National Science & Entrepreneurship Development Board (NSEDB) and National Entrepreneurship Development Board (NEDB) were created under the Chairmanship of the Prime Minister and Union Minister for Industry respectively. Two national resource institutions, i.e., National Institute for Entrepreneurship & Small Business Development (NIESBUD) at New Delhi and Entrepreneurship development Institute of India (EDII) at Ahmedabad were established during the same period. Presently more than 700 organisations including 7 state level entrepreneurship development institutes, 27 SISIs under SIDO, 17 TCOs, 20 Engineering and Technical Institution, 7 STEOs and a host of non-governmental organisations are engaged in developing entrepreneurship. SIDO alone has trained more than 50,000 potential entrepreneurs during 78-88 and one Centre for

Entrepreneurship Development of Gujarat trained more than 10,000 potential entrepreneurs since its inception. In this way thousand of people get opportunities to be developed as entrepreneurs. But the coverage is still far less as compared to the potential available in the country. We may have to took into the infrastructural facility, availability and accessibility to information and technology and develop enormously large cader of trainers and poromoters to reach both urban and rural population. To illustrate, during the 8th Five Year Plan, as per the modest calculations, the country needs about 13,000 trainers, promoters for training potential entrepreneurs as against few hundred which are available today.

The mid 70s witnessed the crystallisation of an integrated model for Entrepreneurship Decelopment (EDP), consisting of stimulatory, support and sustaining activities. This was replicated and very widely with minor variations. The present decade is shaping up to be "age of entrepreneurial explosion". It is visiable as a significant programme in national development plan. During 80s, the structure and function needed for promoting entrepreneurship have become more or less clear. With growing emphasis by the Government and the matching enthusiasm by NGOs, entrepreneurship has now attained the status of a movement.

The movement of entrepreneurship development in India, however, started as part of the total strategy of small industry development. The dynamic SSI policy has strongly supported the cause of entrepreneurship development and both have mutually supplemented each other.

Presently, Small Scale Industries in India are defined by investment limit of Rs. 6 million (Rs. 7.5 million for ancillary units). Besides manufacturing, services, maintenance and processing enterprises are also included in SSI. The tiny sector which has been given the distinctive position is defined as consisting of those units having investment less than Rs. 0.5 million.

The response to such dynamic policy has been very rewarding. The growth of SSI Sector has been one of the most impressive. Between 1973-74 and 1986-87 the number of SSI increased by over 3 folds from 0.416 million to nearly 1.457 million. Presently (1990) their number is estimated as 1.7 million. Employment in this sector has risen more than double from nearly 3.47 million to 10.14 million. The value of Production in terms of current prices increased ten times (Rs. 72,000 million to Rs. 722,500 million). In the field of export, SSI conribution was recorded as approximately 30 per cent of the country's total exports.

More impressive than these statistics is the number crossing 5,000 products which are manufactured in the small scale sector. Beginning with the production of simple consumer goods, the small scale today manufacturs several sophisticated, precision items using latest technology. Some of the sophisticated items precision items using latest technology. Some of the sophisticated items produced in SSI sector include T.V., electronic disk calculator, micro-wave components, electro-medical equipment, miniature bulbs, optical lens, digital measuring equipments, air-conditioning equipments, electric motors, machine tools, authomobile and scooter parts.

Small enterprises in India were also found more economical than large enterprises in terms of capital investment and development generation. Further, small enterprises are providing learning ground for imparting, managerial, entrepreneurial and technical skills. They also provide an outlet for creative urge among individuals to persue excellence in product design and innovations resulting into competitive culture and problem solving orientation which usually lack at the initial stage of development but are basic to socio-economic prosperity.

The most significant aspect of small industry development is that this sector has stimulated vigorously the economic activity of a far reaching magnitude and created a sense of confidence among very large number of small entrepreneurs about their strength and vitality.

FERA being replaced

In keeping with the cuntry's progress towards a more open economy with greater trade and investment linkages with the rest of the world, Mr. Chidambaram said he would introduce later in the year a new Act to replace the Foreign Exchange Regulation Act. 1973 (FERA). At the same time, he signalled a move toward convertibility of the rupee on capital account with his decision to ask the Reserve Bank to set up an expert group to lay out the road map and work out a time table for achieving the goal. A beginning in agricultural sector reform has also been made with the decision to repeal regulations governing rice milling and ginning and pressing factories. Domestic future trading is to be resumed in ginned and baled cotton, raw jute and jute goods.

In formulating his tax proposals, Mr. Chidambaram set himself a target of increasing the net tax revenues of the Centre by 15 to 16 per cent in 1997—98. Notwithstanding the rate reductions and reliefs he has extended, the Finance Minister hopes to make up the loss by better collections. For the corporate sector, he has not only reduced the tax rate to 35 per cent but also abolished the tax on dividends in the hands of the share holder. He, however, proposed a 10 per cent tax on profits distributed in order to persuade companies to invest them for future growth.

Mr. Chidambaram rejected the demand for withdrawal of the controversial Minimum Alternate Tax (MAT) he introduced last year but announced exemption of export profits from MAT. He has also revised the manner in which MAT is charged and collected with a provision for tax credit. He has accepted the Corporate Sector's demand for buy—back of shares by companies and said an overall ceiling of 60 per cent will be kept for intercorporate investment and loans. Another proposal to boost the capital market is a one—time permission to stock brokers to corporatise their business without attracting tax on capital gains which will be exempted.

Tariff reforms

After an interval of one year, Mr. Chidambaram has taken up tariff reform reducing the peak rate of customs duty from 50 to 40 per cent. In the process, he reduced import duty on products which are inputs of the steel industry like coking coal, or on items which would help industries like engineering, textiles, chemicals and host of items related to information technology. The Power sector will get relief with the cut in the duty on non—coking coal from 20 to 10 per cent. In excise duty, Mr. Chidambaram has sought to simplify the structure with three new rates of 8, 13 and 18 per cent, rationalising the existing rates in the process.

The only tax measure in the budget is a tax on certain services calculated to yield Rs. 900 crore in 1997—98 and Rs. 1200 crore in a full year. The net gain to the Centre will however, be only Rs. 300 crore because of the lowering of the interest tax on banks, which would result in a loss of revenue of Rs. 600 crore.

Despite the burdens thrown by the Fifth Pay

Commission recommendations, higher provisions for subsidies, defence and interest payments, Mr. Chidambaram has managed to bring about a reduction in revenue deficit from 2.3 per cent of G.D.P. in the current year to 2.1 per cent next year. He has also increased the budget support for the Central Plan outlay by Rs. 6000 crore.

Mr. Chidambaram has framed his budget against the background of an economy which has been growing at an average rate of 7 per cent during the last three years. He is confident that GDP growth will be sustained at this level or even improved upon in the coming year, though he has listed some areas of concern. These are the sharp decline in crude oil production, poor performance of power sector, the slowdown in export growth, rise in the rate of inflation and volatile capital market. He asserts that his budget proposals are aimed at addressing these concerns. To maintain price stability, he has expressed his determination to adhere toa prudent fiscal policy, contain growth of money supply within 16 per cent and resort to liberal imports of wheat and other essential commodities to counter the pressure on prices. The coming months would show how far the Finance Minister's expectations including price stability (are) are fulfilled. He has indeed given a kick start to an economy which had been widely perceived to have begun to falter in recent months.

Application for collaboration approval

All foreign investment proposals and technical license agreements require approval from either the Secretariat of Industrial Approval (SIA) or the Reserve Bank of Inida (RBI) depending on the applicable criteria.

Applications for approval of technical collaborations requiring clearance by Reserve Bank should henceforth be made in form FC(RBI) (10 copies) to the Controller

Exchange Control Department, Foreign Investment and Technology Transfer Section, Reserve Bank of India, Central Office, Bombay -400 023. Applications requiring clearance of the Government of India should be submitted in form FC(SIA) (10 copies) to the Entrepreneurial Assistance Unit of the Secretariat for Industrial Approvals (SIA) in the Department of Industrial Development, Ministry of Industry, Government of India, Udyog Bhawan, New Delhi - 110 011. Copies of both the Forms along with the guidelines issued by the Reserve Bank of India have been annexed ot this Update so as to assist the reader in knowing the type of information that would have to be supplied to the Indian Authorities.

Following the statement that permission to bring in technology and/or equity participation has been made 'automatic', several notifications and clarifications have been announced by the Government and by Reserve Bank of India regarding the procedural requirements prior to securing such permission. These announcements and policy changes continue to be announced on a day to day basis. Before advising a client or embarking upon a new foreign investment related project, it may therefore be appropriate to seek professional advice and assistance.

Foreign Investment Promotion Board

A specially empowered board namely the Foreign Investment Promotion Board (FIPB) has been constituted and has been vested with enough flexibility to examine those offers that do not come under the purviews of either the RBI or the SIA on a case by case basis. This board, located in the office of the Prime Minister has as its Chairman the Principal Secretary to the Prime Minister. The objective of the Board is to invite and facilitate investment in India by international companies in projects which are considered to be of benefit to the

Indian economy and do not fall within the parameters of the existing policy for clearance of foreign investment proposals. The Board will provide a single window clearance for all aspects of projects considered by it.

The Investment Week issue of November 16, 1992 reports that the Foreign Investment Promotion Board has recently cleared 23 more foreign Investment proposals, most of which are 100% Export Oriented Units, (EOUS) and in the small scale sector.

The investment proposals to the FIPB can be in the form of a plain letter, without any prescribed format and will be decided on the basis of the relevant details given. According to the Government's statement in the Lok Sabha on 15th July, 1992 the criteria for clearing these cases are export potential, employment potential and other benefits likely to accure from the projects. It has been reported that almost all the cases submitted to the SIA and the FIPB in the last few months have received the necessary approvals expeditiously.

Automatic Approval of Foreign Investment and Technology Transfer

The FITT section was set up in the Central Office of the Exchange Control Department at Bombay on 16th September, 1991.

Till 26th September 1992 the FITT had received 996 applications of which 733 were approved and 221 returned for want of certain prerequisites and stipulated conditions being fulfilled by applicants.

The bulk of foreign investments approved were in the chemicals industry, electricals/electronics, food processing, industrial machinery and scientific and electrical laboratory equipment.

Cabinet Committee on Foreign Investment (CCFI)

Proposals involving equity investment over Rs. 3000/- million are submitted to and approved by the CCFI which is headed by the Prime Minister.

A new liberalised policy pakage for the garments sector has been approved at a meeting of the CCFI. The new policy will also enable the garments sector unit to raise its capacity through technologies upgradation and increase investment upto Rs. 30 million provided it exports half of its production.

Opening of Branch Offices in India

The Reserve bank of India in January, 1992 liberalised the branch licensing policy for foreign banks after nearly two decades. Foreign banks have sought 44 more branches as a result.

Foreign companies engaged in the manufacturing and trading activities abroad are now permitted to open branch offices in India for carrying on certain activities as follows:

— to represent the parent company/other foreign companies in various matters in India eg. as buying/selling agents in India etc;

— to conduct research work in which the parent company is engaged provided the results of the research are made available to the Indian companies;

— to undertake export and import trading activities;

— to promote possible technical & financial collaborations between the Indian companies & overseas companies.

Industry-wise update

A brief industry wise Update of the changes in some key industries is given to the next page:

Electronics/computers: Software

The Government of India has recently notified the electronic hardware technology park (EHTP) scheme for building a strong electronics industry with emphasis on enhancing its export potential. For this purpose, foreign equity upto 100% has been allowed in the case of such units. Such a park can be set up by the Central Government, State Governments and public or privates sector organisations. Multinational companies, setting up manufacturing facilities in computer hardware and peripherals under 100% EOU Scheme will be allowed to sell upto 30% of their production in the domestic market. These companies will be allowed to import, paying upto a maximum of 30% import duty, raw materials, plant and machinery.

The following are the recently announced procedural measures initiated by the Government for the delicensing and decentralising of the Electronics Sector:

— The entire electronic industry has been exempted from the locational limitations imposed on other industries and may thus be located even in urban areas.

— Licensing has been abolished for all industrial undertakings including companies covered under Monopolies and Restrictive Trade Practices (MRTP) and Foreign Exchange Regulation Act (FERA) except the sub-sector of consumer electronics and strategic electronics.

— The system of phased manufacturing programme (PMP) run on case by case basis has been abolished.

lDevelopment of small scale industries is being encouraged. Approvals/registrations have been totally decentralised to the level of State Directorates of Industries. Investment limit for this sector has

been revised upwards to Rs. 60 lakhs and that for ancillary units to Rs. 75 lakhs.

— Existing units are permitted to manufacture any article without additional investment under broad-banding subject to certain conditions.

— As recently as 20th November, 1992 the Commerce Ministry has by a notification significantly liberalised the advance licensing scheme for the electronics sector. The Government has substantially reduced and rationalised the value addition norms as well as input output norms for various electronic items, particularly components, with a view to boosting electronic exports from the country.

Software

As India tries to integrate with the world economy some major changes affecting the Indian Software Industry have been initiated by the Government of India.

— Software industry is a 'high priority industry', thus it qualifies for automatic approval by the RBI for 'foreign technology agreements'.

— In March 1992, the Indian Department of Electronics (DOE) authorised the reproduction of foreign software for distribution within India if the local distribution fulfils certain conditions.

— The new Import-Export Policy has substantially eliminated import licensing, quantitative restrictions and other regulatory and discriminatory controls on the import of software.

Tax benefits for the software industry

In order to boost Software exports, the Government of India in the Union Budget 1991-92 has provided a new section whereby an assessee engaged in the business of export of computer software or rendering of technical software services outside India is allowed a pro-rata deduction for the next 3 assessment years. The pro-rata deduction is computed on a formula which takes into consideration the percentage of revenue earned from the export division. If the total income of a software business is generated from exports only, 100% exemption from income tax would be available. This exemption supplements the deduction available in respect of export profits under section 80 HHC of the Income Tax Act 1961.

India's Interest in Setting up Joint Ventures Abroad

The Government of India has consistently been in favour of establishing maintaining and steadily improving economic and technical cooperation among the developing countries and has been adopting all necessary measures for achieving these objectives, duly participating in, and promoting, the global developments of extending the frontiers of international trade and investment.

The problems in industrial development initially faced by India were similar to those faced by most other developing nations, namely, scarcity of capital, low productivity, slow rate of economic growth, absence of infrastructural facilitiess, a rapidly expending population, unemployment, inflation and other socio-economic problems. India has already achieved a considerable measure of success in resolving these during the preceding four decades or so (since the country attained independence) and is tackling the residuary problems with its sagacious economic and industrial policies, modifying in inproving them from time to time, to suit the emerging requirements of the changing times. These resilient and dynamic policies have been aimed at achieving a rapid and orderly industrialisation of the country and a steady improvement in the standard of living of its people. From self-reliance to exporting goods and services India has treaded a long path.

India's achievements on the industrial front by following such policies have been impressive. Besides increase in the volume of industrial output, there has been substantial change in the composition of industrial production over the years. India now produces machinery for textiles, sugar, cement, jute, paper etc. Apart from these, large quantities of metallurgical and heavy equipment and mining machinery are also produced. India has also gone into production of heavy electrical equipment such as power turbines and generators. Substantial capacities have been set up for the production of electric motors of different kinds, as also of various types of machine tools including high-speed lathes, milling machines, radial drills, grinding machines etc. A variety of scientific instruments are also produced.

Top priority accorded to the development of infrastructural facilities over the years has resulted in the establishment of an efficient transportatin and communication network. India has a excellent railway system, which ranks third in the world in terms of route length as well as passenger and goods traffic. There is also a very good network of roads which connects most of the villages and towns. Moreover, the communication system is well-developed and India is connected with most other countries, especially the commercial centres of the world, by modern means of communication.

There has also been tremendous growth in the financial infrastructure. Commercial banking and financial markets, especially in industrial finance, have expanded at very fast rate.

India is in aposition to offer appropriate technologies to other developing countries which are cost-effective, suited to local conditions, make maximum use of local inputs and provide maximum employment to local persons through labour orientation. Some well-known examples are the export of technology for the manufacture of trucks, three wheelers and two wheelers and pulp and paper plants.

According to reliable estimates, more than one thousand consultancy firms, besides individual professionals, are offering their services in various fields. The services offered range from preparation of market surveys, feasibility reports etc. to basic and detailed engineering services, erection and commissioning of plants, training of personnel etc.

The Indian Consultancy Organisations are today offering their services in divergent fields like engineering industries, electronic industries, ferrous and non-ferrous metallurgical industries, chemical industries, aluminium, pulp and paper, forest-based industries, mining and allied industries, urban development, sewage disposal and effluent treatment, distillation and refinery plants, chemical plants, drugs and pharmaceuticals, generation, transmission and distribution of power, railways, highways and bridges, water supply and town planning architecture and irrigation and flood control management.

The Indian enterprises have acquired necessary capabilities of offering project export services ranging from civil and construction projects to industrial projects. The scope of services varies from sub-contracting to execution of turnkey projects. In the industrial sector, the project exports from India range from low level technology areas like structural engineering and power distribution to sophisticated technology areas such as power generation, setting up of chemical plants, cement plants, transportation and tele-communication. In addition to securing a number of project contracts from the countries of West Asia, South Asia, Africa etc., the Indian industry has been able to obtain contracts for projects funded by the World Bank, the Asian Development Bank. The African Development Bank etc. in a process of competitive bidding.

Specialised services from the Indian Consultancy Organisations are available in the fields of Agriculture and Natural Resources, Energy, Oil and Gas Industry, Management Building, Public Health Engineering and Water Supply and Transport. The specific areas in which India can offer joint ventures is illustrated in Annexure I.

The Indian technology suppliers have to comply with rigorous requirements regafding import of technology, local content etc. They are thus in an advantageous position to understand the requirements and conditions of other developing countries and to adapt themselves to those conditins. The technologies offered by India will also be suited to the economies of scale of other developing countries, in addition to being of low cost. India is now in a position to export technology and services in the aforesaid areas and have many joint ventures not only in the developing but even in the highly industrialised countries.

As on 30th June, 1991 there are 159 Indian Joint Ventures in operation in 42 countries. Out of this 22 are in Europe, 7 in the United States of America, 56 in South East Asia, 24 in South Asia, 17 in West Asia, 29 in Africa and 4 in the Oceania region. Another 65 joint ventures are under various stages of implementation in these countries. Indian joint Ventures are in operation in the following areas.

(a) Engineering Industries

1. Light Engineering
2. Commercial Vehicles

(b) Metallurgical Industries

3. Iron and Steel Products

(c) Chemical Industries

4. Textiles and Allied Products
5. Chemicals and Pharmaceuticals
6. Oil Seed Crushing and Palm Oil Refining
7. Food Products (including soft drinks)
8. Pulp and paer
9. Glass and Glass Products
10. Leather and Rubber Products
11. Cement Products

(d) Other Manufacturing Industries

(e) Service Sector

12. Hotels and Restaurants
13. Consultancy
14. Engineering contracts and construction
15. Trading and Marketing

(f) Other Non-manufacturing Ventures

An illustrative list of areas where India is capable of offering technologies and setting up joint ventures is given below:

Metallurgical industries

- Iron and Steel Castings
- Steel Forgings
- Rolling Mill Rolls
- Steel Rolling Mills

- Steel Wires
- Non-ferrous castings
- Aluminium Extrusion

Industrial machinery

- Rice Mill Machinery
- Sugar Mill Machinery
- Boilers
- Air and Water Pollution Control Equipment
- Power Driven Pumps
- Speed Reduction Units
- Chemical and Pharmaceutical Machinery
- Food Processing Machinery
- Pulp and Paper Making Machinery
- Power Plant Equipment
- Miscellaneous Industrial Machinery

Electrical equipment

- Electric Motors
- Alternators
- Transformers
- Condenser Bushings/Circuit Breakers/Power Capacitors
- Arc Furnaces and Induction Furnaces
- Voltage Regulators
- Electric Fans
- Household Electric Appliances
- Electric Bulbs
- Cables and Conductors

Electronic equipment

- Radios, Tape Recorders, "Two-in-Ones"
- Television Receivers
- Components like Resistors, Capacitors, Transistors and Diodes
- Printed Circuit Boards
- Micro/Mini-Computers
- Computer Software

Transportation

- Trucks, Four Wheelers, Three Wheelers, Two Wheelers, Mopeds
- Automobile Ancillaries
- Diesel Engines
- Crawler Tractors/Dumpers/Loaders
- Bicycles and Bicycle Parts

Agricultural machinery

- Agricultural Tractors and Tillers/Agricultural Implements

Machine tools

- Lathes
- Drilling Machines
- Milling Machines
- Planning Machines
- Wood Working Machinery
- Machine Tools Accessories
- Small Tools/Hand Tools

Mechanical engineering

- Structural Fabrication

- Transmission Line Towers
- Pipes and Tubes
- Typewriters
- Cash Registers
- Sewing Machines
- Bolts/Nuts/Screws/Studs
- Drums and Barrels
- Tin Containers
- Cutlery
- Pressure Cookers
- Aluminium and Steel Furniture/Office Equipment
- Steel Almirahs/Vaults/Safes
- Stoves

Other engineering industries

- Air Conditioners and Refrigerators
- Solar Water Heaters/Solar Cookers
- Mathematical and Survey Instruments
- Energy Meters/Water Meters

Chemical industry

- Bricks and Tiles
- Cement
- RCC/PCC Pipes, Poles and Sleepers
- Glass Containers
- Potassium Chlorate/Sodium Chlorate

Fertilisers

- Carbon Black
- Aromatics and Laboratory Chemicals

- Fine Chemical and Flavours
- Cosmetics
- Soaps and Detergents
- Drugs and Pharmaceuticals
- Dye Stuffs and Dye Intermediates
- Food Processing
- Distilleries
- Soft Drink Bottling Plants
- Vegetable Oil Processing
- Solvent Extraction
- Crockery
- Ceramic Tiles
- Sanitary Wares
- Leather and Leather Products
- Paper, Pulp and Paper Products
- Paints/Enamels/Varnishes
- Rubber Products including Automobile Tyre and Tubes
- Plastic Products
- Viscose Staple Fibre
- Jute Goods
- Textiles/Yarns (Cotton/Blended/Synthetic)
- Readymade Garments
- Wooden Furniture
- Sports Goods
- Stationery Items

Other sectors

- Setting up of Hotels/Hospitals/Diagnostic Centres.

Environmental options for the 21st century

Human activities have pushed our planet to the brink of disaster necessitating a comprehensive global action to retrieve the situation. While exploring newer forms of renewable sources of energy to address the environmental malady, our planners and administrators need to address the most urgent task of improving energy efficiency. The rural areas should depend on minihydel projects and bioenergy as far as possible. A serious and lasting government commitment to the development and use of energy efficient and renewable technologies is the need of the hour.

Like it or not, we find ourselves in a world where we are responsible for each other's well-being. In the last few years of this millennium, difficult questions of social equality, national sovereignty, and individual rights and responsibilities are emerging. A person may be able to afford a large, energy-consumptive automobile, but can the planet afford it? Indeed, the larger question boils down as to how many carbon-emitting automobilies can the planet tolerate without the habitability of the earth being disturbed. At a more mundane level, a couple may desire and be able to support several children, but can the planet afford several children per family? Does our generation have the right to extinguish plant and animal species that have evolved over millions of years? Do we not have the obligation to preserve our biological heritage for our future generations?

An affirmative answer to these questions depends on restoring and prserving the conditions that make the earth habitable, a place capable of supporting a diversity of life and modern civilization. Human activities have pushed the planet to the brink of disaster.

Agenda for action

A comprehensive global action plan to remedy the

situation should include: developing energy strategies that have climate protection as their cornerstone; expanding the earth's forest cover so as to prevent global warming; doubling the per capita grain production and lastly, breaking the momentum of population growth.

While these are the macro-level targets for making this globe a sustainable one in the forthcoming century, at the micro-level it amounts to a severe test on the capacity of world leaders as well as the local ones in their efforts in ecological economic betterment of the populations under their jurisdiction.

It is no wonder that the modes of energy production that are in vogue around the world are primarily responsible for the change in the earth's climate. The huge quantities of oil, coal and natural gas that fuel the global economy account for most of the carbon dioxide emissions responsible for global warming through the greenhouse effect. Producing less carbon dioxide requires using less fuel from among the traditional category. This in turn means exploring other non-conventional energy sources, enough to substitute the fossil sources.

13

Council of Scientific and Industrial Research

The CSIR is the national R&D organisation providing scientific industrial research for India's economic growth and human welfare. It has a country-wide network of forty laboratories and eighty field centres covering fundamental and applied R&D in all areas of science and technology barring atomic research, developing and nurturing S&T human resource for the country through extra mural support and promoting scientific talent through awards, fellowships etc.

As CSIR reorients itself to be market driven and move on the path of self-financing, its performance would be conditioned by the performance of the Indian industry and economy. Thus the rate of ECF generation from contract R&D and consultancy came down from 15 to 10%, the actual ECF going up from Rs. 190 crore to Rs. 209 crore. The contribution to creation of new knowledge was satisfactory, patent filings increased significantly, rising from 71 to 91 in the year for foreign patents and from 209 to 264 for Indian patents. The quality of papers contributed also showed a healthy upward trend although the number remained nearly static. CSIR's all round performance during the year was satisfactory. Most significant among its activities has been the winning initiative for revocation of US patent on turmeric, which besides confirming CSIR's pioneering efforts to successfully safeguard traditional Indian knowledge, created an unprecedented positive pub'ic goodwill for the CSIR. More importantly this success had some far-reaching effects viz: it demonstrated that CSIR and other Indian institutions were acquiring capabilities to fight the complex techno-legal issues of IPR, both defensively and aggressively, to meet the challenges under the WTO regime; it showed the importance of appropriate documentation and public availability of records of traditional knowledgebase in a systematic manner, which can be provided as evidence of prior knowledge; it reassured the Indian people of the fair and transparent operations of the IPR system.

Scientific and technological achievements

The S&T Contributions from CSIR are of value to almost all socio-economic sectors. CSIR carries out R&D and provides services of value not only industry but also to other sectors of the economy e.g. agriculture, health, energy, rural development, transport and defence. CSIR's help to domestic industry is not only by way of relevant/ competitive technologies but also through search of raw materials and components, pollution control, productivity enhancement etc. A few of the more significant achievements during the year are reported through the charts and write-up given herein

Bio-sciences Including Therapeutics

Scientific achievements

Regulation of cell growth

In studies on the cell cycle regulated protein tyrosine phosphatases, CCMB has reported that over expression of PTP-S2 shortens the duration of S-phase (DNA replication) suggesting thereby that the duration of DNA replication is being reduced in these cells. It was also seen that over expression of PTP-S2 in Cos 1 cells resulted in cell death by apoptosis in about 30% of transfected cells after 48 hours.

Liposome entrapped mite allergen

Liposomes, which are non-toxic biodegrdable and biocompatible lipid vesicles are known to act as adjuvant and antigen materials and can be attached to the cuter surface or encapsulated within the internal aqueous spaces. CBT studies aimed at further evaluating liposcmes containing mite (Dermatophagoids farinae) in different strain of mice, confirm the immuno-adjuvant effect of liposome for immunotherapy in allergic disorders. These studies lead to the conclusion that increase in formation of protecting antibodies IgG and at the same time decrease in specific IgE. Using Liposome Entrapped Allergen (LEA) reduces the risk of systemic reaction associated with conventional allergy immunotherapy.

Functional studies of lectins

In symbiosis, soil microbes (Genus, Rhizobium) infect leguminous plants to form root nodules where bacteria inhabit and fix atmospheric nitrogen for the plant, and in return the plants supply food (sugar) to bacteria. The first step for this pleasant dwelling together is the selection of right partner. It has been proposed by many groups, including CBT that bacterial polysaccharides interact with root lectins specificaNy and that is the basis for recognition of correct partners. CBT has now experimentally demonstrated how the root lectin (PRA II) interacts with specific rhizobial polysaccharides.

Tumour biology

CCMB is studying the mechanisms involved in the spontaneous regression of a rat histiocytoma, AK-5 in syngeneic hosts. The tumor rejection antigen from the cDNA library developed from the tumor was cloned. The fusion protein from this clone is immunogenic and renders the animals partially resistant to tumor challenges. The nature of this antigen is being studied further to understand its immunological behaviour and to study the physiological function of the protein.

Brain cytochrome P450(s) enzymes

Studies conducted at ITRC have shown evidence of multiple forms of cytochrome P450 using specific antibodies and enzyme activity in different parts of rat brain. A commonly used pesticide, deltamethrin in coils and mats for mosquito control was found to enhance the activity of brain 7-pentoxyresorufin O-dealkylase (PROD). Prolonged exposure to the pesticide resulted in a significant increase in the activity of brain (EROD 1.3 fold) as well. The addition of anti-P450 antibody in 2B 1/2132 in vitro to the reaction mixture inhibited the enzyme activity of PROD upto 80%, whereas no inhibition was observed in EROD activity when compared to the control where pre-immune IgG was added. The results suggest that deltamethrin preferentially induces isoenzymes involved in the metabolism of deltamethrin and the role of P450 2B I/ 2B2 mediated metabolism in the neurotoxicity of pesticide.

New approaches in chemotherapy of malaria

It is known that intra-erythrocytic proliferation of malaria parasite is mainly responsible for pathogenesis and pathology of malaria infection. Recent studies at CDRI have demonstrated two distinct biochemical targets for antimalarial drug action:

a) The process of heme polymerisation whereby the malaria parasite converts hemoglobin to free toxic heme and finally to a polymeric detoxified product called hemozoin which is necessary for growth and survival of the parasite. A novel reaction initiated by blood schizontocidal antimalarials causing depolymerisation of hemozoin has been identified, as a result compounds specifically inhibiting this process may provide novel effective antimalarials.

b) Stage specific increase in polyamine levels (spermine, spermidine and putrescine), present only in traces in normal erythrocytes, was observed during growth and multiplication of malaria parasite in intraerythrocytic schizogony. Parasite induced putrescine transport system was highly specific and was inhibited by compounds interfering with polyamine biosynthesis. This provides an effective strategy for development of new chemotherapeutic molecules against malaria.

Rapid screen for anti-TB drugs

Recombinant Mycobacterium aurum A+, a fast growing non-pathogenic strain, expressing Escherichia coli lacZ gene has been constructed at CDRI, with -galactosidase as the reporter system. A good correlation was observed between inhibition in -galactosidase production and growth of recombinant strain by anti-TB drugs. The assay is highly predictive of activity against M. tuberculosis.

Molecular epidemiology of Cholera

In the study on molecular epidemiology of cholera IMT in collaboration with NICED, Calcutta has been able to empirically establish that the clones of V cholerae 01 or 0139 emerge, purge the existing clones and then spread spatially in waves and that the genetic flux in the V cholerae aids in the process. It also showed that the new clone of V. cholerae which appeared in Calcutta in September 1993 migrated to Guinea-Bissau within a year and was responsible for the epidemic which began in 1994 there.

Drug induced gastric hyperacidity

IICB had earlier shown that mercaptomethylimidazone (MMI) an anti thyroid drug of thiomide group, is a potent inducer of gastric acid secretion. While studying the mechanism it was observed that the system of isolated parietal cell activate the for acid secretion. H_2O_2, generated by inactivation of the H_2O_2, degrading enzymes can also stimulate acid secretion in the isolated gastric mucosal and gastric gland preparations. The plausible role of H_2O_2 acting like a second messenger to activate the parietal cell has thus been suggested.

Molecular studies on Cytoplasmic Male Sterility

The cytoplasmic male sterility (CMS) in plants has been exploited in the seed industry for the production of improved hybrid seeds. A rice mitochondrial gene orfl 55, characterised at NBRI showed altered transcript size between CMS and maintainer lines. The nucleotide sequence of the gene cloned from mitochondrial genome was compared with that of cDNA of the corresponding transcript. The orfl 55 posseses 7 editing sites in both the CMS and the maintainer lines.

Plant pathogens

(i) Bacterial infection of rice: CCMB continued the studies on the interaction between the rice plant and the bacterial pathogen Xanthomonas oryzae pv. Oryzae (Xoo), and reports that incorporation of both the xa-13 and xa-21 resistance genes into susceptible rice cultivars might provide broad-based protection against Xoo.

(ii) Microbial resistance to-plant antibiotics: studies on the response of Dictyostelium to isoflavonoid phytoalexins has enabled CCMB to propose a novel plant-microbe interaction between leguminous plants and cellular slime moulds. The leguminous plant uses isoflavonoid compounds to manipulate the foraging behaviour of amoebae so as to get rid of potentially pathogenic rhizosphere bacteria from the vicinity of root lesions,

DNA marker for papaya sex identification

In papaya, where male and female plants are separate, a method has been developed to identify sex at seedling stage. The method involved identification of male specific DNA marker using microsatellites as well as RAPD primers.

Somatic embryogenesis in Mango

NCL has succeeded in achieving direct somatic embryogenesis and plantlet regeneration in economically important monoembryonic mango varieties viz. Alphonso,

Mundan and Baneshan. The plants have been transferred to field. Long term repetitive somatic embryogenesis have also been obtained which is an important step towards scaling up of protocols. The achievement is significant as complete plantlet have been obtained and field planted.

Azadirachtin and limonoids in the Indian neem tree

A detailed investigation was carried out by CIMAP to document the variation in azadirachtin, nimbin, nimbidin and salanin contents during growth of neem seeds in different agro-climatic zones of India depending upon temperature, humidity and altitude. It has been observed that the percentage of all these limonoids in the seeds keep on increasing right from the formation of fruit fill the maturity of the seeds and biosynthesis of these limonoids is very fast while the fruit is being converted from green to the ripe, thereafter the increase is slow, and slightly declines when the fruit is about to fall or has just fallen from the tree suggesting that harvesting at the time of maturity is beneficial.

Antibacterial activity of Indian tree species

CIMAP evaluated the fruits and seeds of three-tree species namely Indian walnut (Albizia lebbeck), drum stick (Moringa oleifera), and Indian beech (Pongamia pinnata) using tissue discs or fragments directly for antibacterial activity against three bacteria: Salmonella typhimurium, Pseudomonas aeruginosa and Mycobacterium smegmatis (non-pathogenic soil saprophyte spp.). The results indicate the presence of a highly potential anti-mycobacterial compound in the extracts of Moringa (drumstick) fruit.

Marine fouling and corrosion studies

Extracts of two terrestrial plants belonging to the family Leguminoceae and Lecythidaceae studied by NIO were found to exhibit potent antifouling activity against some important fouling organisms.

Technological achievements

Universal polymer support for synthesis of oligoribonucleotides

Solid phase synthesis of DNA and RNA requires at least eight different prederivatised polymer supports. The commercial availability of base labile synthons for DNA and RNA synthesis has necessitated the need to prepare a large number (50-60) of such pre-derivatised polymer supports making DNA and RNA synthesis a time consuming task. CBT has developed a versatile universal polymer support devoid of nucleotidic material and compatible to the existing methods of synthesis and deprotection of oligodeoxyribo and oligobionucleotides. The universal support obviates the need to prepare a large number of pre-derivatised polymer supports. Patent has been applied for the development in India and USA.

Diagnostic probe for leishmaniasis

A probe for early detection of visceral leishmaniasis has been developed at CDRI, by using a pair of oligonucleotide primers constructed from predominant sequence class of kinetoplast DNA minicircle of leishmania donovani. An Indian patent has been filed for the development.

Assay for Acute Lymphoblastic Leukemia (ALL)

Childhood acute lymphoblastic leukemia or 'ALL' requires prolonged maintenance therapy for eliminating residual leukemic blast cells which cannot be detected by standard morphological methods. These persisting cells are responsible for relapse and is called 'Minimal Residual Disease' (MRD). Employing a unique 9-0-acetylated sialic acid binding lectin (ATNH), two 9-0 acetyl sialoglyconjugates (9-OacSGs) on lymphoblasts have been identified by IICB. 'A lymphoproliferative assay which is selective for PBMC of 'ALL' and not of other blood disorders has been developed.

Human trial of a non-toxic cholera vaccine

CSIR developed indigenous and genetically engineered

oral cholera vaccine named Val -3 has been cleared for human trials by the Drug Controller. This development has been the result of a collaborative project between IMT, IICB and NICED, Calcutta and is based on a non-reactogenic natural isolate of V cholerae 01.

Novel usage of di-tert-butyl polycarbonate (DTBP)
IICT has been successful in utilizing DTBP for cyclodehydration of n-acylamino acids to substituted oxazoles and enantiopure synthesis of bioactive alkyl amino benzoxazinones which are effective protease inhibitors. Currently, DTBP is used for introduction of acid labile BOC protecting group in amino acids, peptides and proteins.

Isovitamin C by a genetically altered organism
A fermentation process for the production of 2-keto-gluconate - a penultimate intermediate of isoascorbic acid (Isovitamin C) used as antioxidant for the preservation of food products has been developed by RRL -Jammu. The laboratory has demonstrated the process at 500 litre scale to a firm in Hyderabad. The Chemostat studies on the genetically modified Pseudomonas clone revealed 40% increase in the productivity of 2-keto-gluconate. The organism mediating the glucose oxidation process has been improved by cloning another set of glucose dehydrogenase derived from Acinetobacter calcoaceticus.

Mini Chrysanthemum—CV. Mother Teresa
A new chrysanthemum cultivar, selected from open pollinated seedlings, named "Mother Teresa" was released by NBRI. It is a small flowered, white Anemone type mini chrysanthemum which has all the qualities to occupy a high position in floriculture trade. It requires neither 'Pinching' nor 'Staking'. It can easily be transported in small containers due to its mini habit.

Application of chloro choline chloride for bulb production of Tulips

IHBT has shown that chloro choline Chloride treatment at the early stage of flower emergence increases the bulb yield per plant by nearly 50%, bulb weight by over 100%, bulb size (circumference) about 20%, bulblet production by 30% and weight of bulblets over 50% as compared to the untreated plants.

Ocimum carnosum, a potential source of natural elemicin

Elemicin is highly valued in the pharmaceutical industry besides being an important flavouring agent. It is the base material for the production of 3,4,5 trime thoxy benzaldehyde and is also a starting material for the synthesis of trimethoprim, an ingredient used in the formulation of anti-bacterial drugs. A valuable elemicin source is the herb Ocimum carnosum, which RRL-Jammu has established and developed for commercial cultivation.

New varieties of damask rose

IHBT has released two new cultivars of Damask Rose designated as IHBT, Gulab-I (Jwala) and IHBT Gulab-II (Himroz) during the year. Jwala is suitable for sub-tropical plains and mid hills upto 1400 in altitude while Himroz is suitable for temperate zone upto 2500 in altitude.

Production technology for rose oil and rose water

CIMAP has developed a low cost and efficient technology for the production of rose oil and water. A directly fired type rose oil distillation plant of 150 kg flower capacity was designed, fabricated and installed at village Devnagar in Ajmer (Rajasthan). The composition of the major constituents of the rose oil produced with Pushkar (Rajasthan) rose as determined by the GLC has been found to be at par with the composition of the rose oil produced from the flowers of Rosa damascena grown by CIMAP in Kashmir.

Tissue Culture for Licorice and Ashwagandha

Tissue culture studies were under taken by NCL for

propogation of Neem (Azadirachta indica) and Licorce *(Glycryrrhiza glabra), Ashwagandha (Withania somnifera)* using different pathways like micropropogation, direct and indirect induction of somatic embryogenesis and induction of secondary metabolites from callus cultures, Protocols for mass production were developed for Licorice and Ashwagandha. The technique has tremendous potential for selection of variants adoptable to extreme conditions.

Plant transformation technology

NCL developed plant transformation technology for improved chickpea and pigeonpea and also standardized protocols on regeneration of whole plants from various explants via somatic embryogenesis and organogenesis.

Biodegradation of endosulfan from contaminated sons

A two-member bacterial coculture has been isolated at ITRC from contaminated soil that biodegrades alpha and beta isomers of endosulfan. Degradation of alpha and beta-endosulfan was 18% and 27% respectively in uninoculated conditions and by inclusion this was enhanced to nearly 75% for both the isomers. Biodegradation also caused substantial reduction in the toxicity of endosulfan as tested by ecotoxicity protocols. Another bacterial strain ITRC- I degraded all four isomers of HCH in flooded conditions, showing formation of 2,5-dichlorophenol by thin layer chromatography technique.

Wildlife management by genetic fingerprinting

(1) Genetic diversity in Indian big cats: studies at CCMB have led to the identification of Asiatic lions and tigers with high genetic variability which could be used for front line breeding. Also, observations of the Indian big cat species suggest that low genetic variability may be a characteristic feature rather than the result of intensive inbreeding as commonly thought.

(2) Fertility status of lions, tigers and leopards in India:

CCMB has established the fertility status of the male cats based on the semen profiles and hormonal levels. Lions (8), tigers (2 1) and leopards (15) from the Nehru Zoological Park, Hyderabad, the Sakkarbaug Zoo, Junnagadh and the Nandankanan Zoo, Bhubaneshwar have been successfully electroejaculated and the semen characteristics such as motility, viability, sperm number and morphology among others, were evaluated.

Chemical sciences and technology

Scientific achievements

Liquid Membrane Modelling

RRL-Jorhat in association with C-MMACS developed a mathematical model incorporating external mass transfer across the aqueous boundary layer and interfacial chemical reaction and diffusion in the emulsion globule. The model has been validated through a computer simulation exercise describing the experimental extraction kinetics of various cephalosporin antibiotics in an optimised liquid membrane system.

Pillaring of ion-exchanged clays

NCL has employed a novel, ultrasonic technique to regulate and accelerate the pillaring process. In this method, the process of pillaring of alumina and zirconia is complete within a matter of few hours with minimum or no elimination of the partent clay. The conditions, the concentration of pillaring species and the frequency of ultra-sonication have been optimised to achieve alumina and zirconid pillared clays (montmorillonite) which also showed much better thermal and hydrothermal stabilities than reported before.

Transition metal complexes with designed ligands

CSMCRI in continuation of the ongoing effort to design transition metal complexes with specific properties synthesised and characterised the following:

a) Polypyridyl complexes to study energy transfer processes: hetero bi and tri-nuclear metal complexes of Ru (III)/(II) and Fe (II) incorporating the ligands, pyridyl derivatives of ferrocene, polycarboxylic acids (edta) and 2,2' - bipyridyl were synthesised. All these new complexes showed a moderate to weak electrochemical interaction between the redox centre. A series of mono nuclear ru. (3)-polypyridyl triazine) complex synthesised showed excellent catalytic property towards electrocatalytic reduction of carbon dioxide to formic acid.

b) Coordination polymer for adsorption: a series of polymeric Co(II) and Cu(II) complexes using adipic acid as bridging ligand and 2,2' -bipyridyl as terminal ligand were synthesised and characterised crystallographically. Analysis of the structures show strong intra and inter molecular H-bonding interactions forming two-dimensional network structures.

c) Biomimitic molecular models: dinuclear Cu(II) complexes of diethylenetriamine, using dicarboxylato and substituted imidazolato ligands as spacer between the metal centres and also some schiff base complexes were synthesised as model systems.

d) Thermochromic materials: a number of Ni(II) and Cu(II) complexes with the ligands dialkyl-/tetraalkyl-ethylenediamine and diazaclothep-tane with various anions have been synthesised and characterised crystallographically. These complexes exhibit thermochromic transitions (reversible colour change) at liquid nitrogen temperature. The variable temperature single crystal X-ray studies of some samples and the latice energy computations for the molecular motions involved in the crystal during transition were carried out in collaboration with IICT.

New chemical entities

IICT has focussed research efforts on development of novel synthetic molecules with significant level of biological activity for possible applications in drugs/ pharmaceuticals, agrochemicals and performance products. Notable among the molecules taken up are Gonio furfurones, Epothilines/ amphidinolides, Azamacrolides [optically active], Macrocyclic lactones, Glycopeptides, Sugar aminoacids, 2-Tetra zolyl-3-aryl propanols.

Synthesis of N-protected precursors of synthetic sweetener aspartame

N-protected derivatives of L-aspartyl-L-phenylalanine methyl ester are useful as precursors of synthetic sweetener : Aspartame which is 200 times sweeter than sugar and used in industry as artificial sweetener in beverages and food additives. Enzyme assisted reaction of N-[benzyloxy carbonyl]-L-aspartic acid [ZASP] or N-[phenylacetyl]-Laspartyl acid [PASP] with L-phenylalanine methyl ester [PME] was achieved by IICT to produce N-[benzyloxycarbonyl]-L-aspartyl-L-phenylalanine methyl ester [Z-aspartame] or N-[phenylacetyl]-L-aspartyl-L-phenylalanine methyl ester [Phaspartame].

Technological achievements

Foam as a reaction medium

The IICT-CCMB joint efforts, have led to the development of foam as an environment friendly reaction medium for enzyme mediated organic reactions. The typical example is lipase catalyzed transformations of aliphatic acids/ alcohols to corresponding esters. The specific advantages of employing foam are, reduced hydrolysis of products and absence of organic solvents. There are good prospects of applying this option for chemical synthesis.

Clay supported new reagents

Clay supported new reagents preparation and their applications in functional group transformations especially under microwaves was an important area of research at IICT. A general method for the synthesis of iso-thiocyanates from dithiocarbamates has been developed using 'clay-cop'. The method is applicable for the preparation of a variety of iso-thiocyanates, including aminoacids. The method avoids the use of toxic chemicals like thio-phosgene and lead nitrate.

Chiral template for enantiomers

Amino acids are of paramount importance in asymmetric synthesis and are used extensively in both the 'chiral substrate' and 'chiral auxiliary' based versions of stereoselective reactions. Under the research programme directed towards the synthesis of enantiopure compounds of biological interest, IICT has developed methods to synthesize a number of bioactive molecules utilizing the easily available amino acids as 'chiral template' to obtain enantiomerically pure compounds of contemporary interest.

Membrane/adsorptive separation

RRL-Jorhat developed liquid membrane process for selective separation of cephalosporin-C from its mixture with de-acetyl cephalosporin-C generated in the fermentation broth of Cephalosporin acremonim.

Oxidative Coupling of Methane (OCM) to C2-Hydrocarbons

A highly stable and active, selective catalyst comprising of alkaline and rare earth oxides supported on low surface area microporous catalysts carriers has been developed at NCL. An energy efficient process for the oxidative coupling of methane to C2-Hydrocarbons over this catalyst using a concept of catalyst dilution by inert solids for exothermic oxidative conversion and endothermic thermal cracking reactions to avoid the hot spot formation and heat removal problems has been developed. The novelty of the process is its reduced hazardous nature.

Isomerization of O-dichlorobenzene to M-dichlorobenzene

The isomerization of O-dichlorobenzene is usually carried out with homogenous catalysts ($FeCl_3$, etc.) which have detrimental effect on the environment with problems of separation. M-dichlorobenzene is a value-added chemical intermediate. NCL has developed a suitable zeolite based catalyst for the isomerization and fixed bed operation. The reaction parameters have been optimized to achieve maximum conversion of odcb and selectivity to mdcb. The novelty in this development is a regenerable catalyst, patented and not reported earlier for such application. The development for an Indian Industry, planning to put up a semi-commercial (pilot) plant of 1000 tons per annum capacity with its own engineering inputs. This will be a non-polluting chemical plant. The development paves way for developing suitable heterogeneous catalysts for isomerization of other organic substrates.

CFC-113a technology for pyrethroids

1,1,1-Trichloro-trifuoroethane [CFC-113a] is a eommercially important synthone for the introduction of a two carbon functionality terminating in trifluoromethyl group in bioactive molecules. The CFC-l13a is a key raw material for producing highly potent and less toxic pyrethroid class of insecticides like lamdacyhalothrin. Its commercial production has become the monopoly of those agencies having access to CFC- 113a. The recent restrictions on the use of CFCs under Montreal Protocol has made its availability difficult for the Indian industry.

IICT has entered into an agreement with a private sector company in Mumbai for development of lamdacyhalothrin and CFC-113a The CFC-113a is made by the catalytic isomerization of CFC-1 13 followed by fractional distillation. The development of process for CFC-113a on pilot scale has been successfully demonstrated on a 3 kg/batch. The requisite catalyst has also been developed by the laboratory.

Electrochemical systems of naphthoquinone

Naphthoquinone (NQ) and its substituted derivatives are

industrially significant as intermediates in the synthesis of anthroquinone, dyes and pharmaceuticals. The current process for the production of NQ and its substituted derivatives is by oxidation of Naphthalene. The yield of NQ in this process is less than 40%. CECRI has developed an electro mediated synthesis route where the purity and yield of NQ are high. Further the process enables the synthesis of number of versatility of industrially important compounds like aldehydes, as well. Electro organic synthesis of NQ is mote convenient, economical and environmental friendly.

Pyridine based chemicals

CFRI successfully demonstrated the process to convert 3-picoline to 3-cyanopyridine and the conversion of 4-cyanopyridine to INH. The maximum yield of 3-cyanopyridine achieved so far is 85% by weight. Zeolite and pillared clay based vanadia catalyst have been prepared and tested for the reaction. Construction of a plant to produce 1 1000 kg per day nicotinamide from 3-cynopyridine is in progress.

Cardanyl Acrylate and Poly Acrylate

RRL-Tvm has standardised process know-how for the laboratory scale production of cardanyl acrylate and poly acrylate. The technology was transferred to a small scale firm.

Pervaporation technology

IICT has acquired specialised expertise in pervaporation technology. It is devising an economically attractive pervaporation process for the separation of paraffins and olefins to upgrade commercial propylene for a company in Visakhapatnam.

Conversion of methane to syngas

An energy efficient and safe to operate process for the methane to syngas (CO and H_2) based on simultaneous partial oxidation, steam reforming and CO_2 reforming of methane over a novel supported nickel catalyst has been developed at NCL. Because of the simultaneously occuring exothermic oxidative conversion and endothermic steam and CO_2 reforming reactions, the process occurs in a most energy efficient and safe manner, requiring little or no external energy. NCL is trying to operate this process in an adiabatic reactor, as the process can be made almost thermoneutral.

Conversion of natural gas to lower olefins

Natural gas contains methane with appreciable amount of C_2-C_4 alkanes. It is practically important to convert the C_{2+} hydrocarbons without their separation from natural gas into ethylene and C_3-C_4 olefines. For this purpose two different processes, one based on the catalytic oxidative conversion of all the hydrocarbons in the presence of a limited oxygen, and the second based on the non-catalytic oxypyrolysis of natural gas in the presence of limited oxygen, have been developed at NCL. In both processes, the exothermic oxidative conversion and endothermic thermal cracking reactions, which are occurring simultaneously, are coupled to make these processes most energy efficient.

Menthol manufacture

A novel technology for the manufacture of menthol from menthol oil has been developed at IIP which gives product of a very high quality at lower processing costs. The technology offers special features of distillation of mentha oil through a more efficient column enabling the higher yield of menthol of high purity meeting international specifications and chemical transformation of menthone to menthol and the isomerisation of undesired to desired isomers of menthol.

Soaker visbreaking technology

IIP has developed a state-of-art indigenous technology for

soaker visbreaking, an improved version of the coil visbreaking, for processing of petroleum residues into more value added products. The technology has been developed in collaboration with EIL and optimised at the pilot level. The technology offers advantages of lower operating temperatures and higher residence time leading to nearly 15% savings in fuel consumption in comparison to the coil visbreaking. Almost all the coil visbreakers in the Indian refineries have been revamped based on the data generated at the IIP pilot plant, besides two grass roots plants being put up.

Mini refinery

IIP has been pioneering the concept of mini refineries for the country. In this direction it has prepared several techno-economic reports for various clients for mini refineries with capacities varying from 0.5 to 2.0 MMTPA. These mini refineries are self contained, skid mounted, low cost and low maintenance units congenial for installation in any location.

Reaction engineering laboratory

The IICT has recently established sophisticated experimental facilities for the development of eivirocatalyzed chemical processes for the speciality chemical sector. Laboratory is equipped with a unique bench scale facility for the standardization of catalyst preparation, full range of physicochemical test facilities for characterization of catalysts [heterogeneous], micro and mini flow reactor with online GO HPLC facilities, reaction calorimeter for standardization of batch processes, accelerated rate calorimeter for assessing the thermal hazards of chemical processes and bench and pilot scale fixed bed reactors with downstream processing facilities.

State-of-art system for chemical reaction studies

IIP has procured a versatile computer controlled general

purpose facility comprising micro reactor and pilot plant system used for conducting scale-up studies of chemical processes. The facility is specially useful for reaction studies in liquid/gas phase over fixed catalyst bed at micro level and as well as at pilot scale at temperatures upto 500°C and upto 50 bar pressure.

Electronics and Instrumentationn

Scientific achievements

Electron cyclotron resonance source plasma

CSIO has developed an electron cyclotron resonance (ECR) system for studying microwave plasma in argon, oxygen, carbon tetrafloride and in a mixture of oxygen and carbon tetrafloride. A cylindrical Langmuir probe was used to measure the current and its variation with respect to input power (50 - 1000W), flow rates, probe position in the reactor and pressure. These measurements give optimum operational parameters. It has been observed that ion current increases linearly with microwave power.

Chemical composition of rainfall: monitor

CSIO studied the rainwater composition at event temporal resolution, over a 6- month period, at a site in south east England. The data were used to assess the overall levels of acidic deposition at the site and to identify functional relationships between wet deposition and casual meteorological processes. It was seen that a power-law relationship existed between wet deposition and rainfall amount. A microprocessor based acid rain monitor designed for the study not only fulfilled requirements of various international bodies but also emerged as basic research tool in the field of acid precipitation studies.

High performance CPU without secondary cache

While undertaking the mammoth project to port and parallelise the T-80 weather prediction code on NAL's parallel computer, Flosolver, it was found that there was a large discrepancy between the advertised peak speed and the realised sustained speed on the intel 1860 processor—a discrepancy which appeared to be general to all RISC processors. Scientists in NAL supported by the CSIR's New Idea Fund (NIF) undertook the project to design a high performance CPU without secondary cache. The basic methodology used was to design the CPU card and RAM interface, develop logical equations, fabricate the printed circuit board, and finally develop, test and analyse the board. The board has now been designed and tested and proved to be functionally working.

Technological achievements

Electrical double layer capacitors (edlc)

Usually non-aqueous solvents are used as electrolytes in edic to achieve voltage windows higher than 1.25V For the first time edic using aqueous alkaline electrolyte with carbon and/or Ni/NiO as electrodes have been fabricated, by CECRI, Button type, coin type and cylindrical type capacitors and capacitor banks have been fabricated and tested.

Solid state room temperature gas sensor

CEERI is using the properties of high Tc cuprate superconductor to detect NH_3 and NO_x gases at room temperature. A Capacitively-Coupled Field Effect Transistor (CCFET) has been developed as a sensor for the purpose which gives a 10mV output for a 5 ppm NH 3 concentration.

Speed indicating and recording instrument for locomotives

A PC-based speed indicating and recording instrument has been developed by CEERI for diesel and electric locomotives in collaboration with a private industry. The performance of the prototype model has been tested on an electric locomotive of Indian Railways. The salient features of the instruments are: non-contact inductive DC type proximity sensor with IP-6 standards, 6 digit odometer with bright LED display, speed indication, full-function key board for initial data entry, data retrieval and data transfer interface/ switch and interactive selection of conditional data for display and analysis. The instrument is useful for indicating and recording relevant train data such as loco speed, time, date etc. in NVROM. The system provides valuable information for locomotive movement and analysis of causes in case of accidents.

Instrumentation for microelectronics

CSIO with the assistance from UNDP and Government counterpart funding from the CSIR and the DoE has successfully developed the following:

a) *Molecular Beam Epitaxy (MBE) System* used for growth of semiconductor epitaxial layers, monolithic microwave integrated circuits (MMICs), very high speed integrated circuits (VHSICs) etc.

b) *Stepper Optical Lithography (SOL)* facility essential for the fabrication of LSI/VLSI devices and ASICs in all microelectronic foundries.

c) *Reactive Ion Beam Etching (RIBE) System* based on ECR source used for etching fine anisotropic patterns for fabricating microelectronic (VLSI/ VHSIC) devices as well as for micromachining and making fine optical gratings.

d) *Reactive Ion Etching (RUE) System* necessary for etching a variety of materials like Silicon, Polysilicon, Silicon Dioxide, Nitrides, Silicides, Group III-V Compound Semiconductors, etc. for fabrication of microelectronic and photonic devices. This system also finds applications in the areas of microfabrication and micromechanics.

e) *RF/DC Sputtering System* which has applications for deposition of thin films in semiconductor industries, optical industries, integrated optics, industrial hard and decorative coatings, etc.

f) *Electron Beam Controlled Evaporation (EBCE)* system for growth/deposition of high quality thin films of different solid materials. It finds wide applications in areas of microelectronics, optics, superconductors, etc.

g) *LSI/VLSI Testing System* for general purpose programmable testing of LSI/VLSI devices as well as for sorting of devices having particular specifications.

RF Hyperthermia system for cancer therapy

Hyperthermia is a new emerging technique for treatment of localised cancers. CSIO has designed and developed a Hyperthermia System at 27 MHz for intracavitary applications in uterine cervix using capacitive type of non-invasive applicator system. A specific control algorithm has been developed for control of temperature measurement.

Receivers for optical communication

CEERI has developed Need Specific Detectors and Receivers for Optical Communication System comprising hybrid optical fron-end module and integrated optical receiver module.

Land based Digital Seismic Data Telemetry System

CSIO in collaboration with NGRI has developed an eight-channel Digital Seismic Data Telemetry System based on state-of-art technology. The system is meant to monitor and analyse micro-earthquakes/earthquakes data telemetered from a network of seismic remote stations via digital ground telemetry down to a central recording and analysis base station. At the base station, the seismic data can immediately be processed and analysed for the purpose of research in the field of earthquake prediction.

Inclinometer probe with digital indicator

CSIO has developed a portable and light weight inclinometer which incorporates special features of high accuracy and ruggedness; excellent stability; water proof stainless steel housing; digital data indicator with 4 1/2 -

digit large LCD display, dust proof enclosure and rechargeable battery.

PC based data acquisition system for thermo physical studies

NAL has successfully developed a PC based data acquisition system for thermophysical studies. The system, built around a temperature controlled furnace with attachments for studying several thermo physical phenomena is available both in the PC based and manual models. The PC based system offers software control of temperature, temperature gradient and the computation of different physical activities.

Engineering

Scientific achievements

Control of Fly-rock due to blasting

A blast mat was indigenously designed, manually weaved and used by CMRI to control fly-rock at a limestone mine. The use of bottom bole initiation, adequate stemming equal to burden and hole to hole delay pattern helped in total control of fly-rock and production of an ideal muck profile. Each blast mat was of 6×6m in dimension and the ropes were interlocked with each other. Elimination of fly-rock using blast mats at the peripherial areas of this mine generated scope of cost reduction by minimising ripping and dozing operations which accounted for 20-25 percent of the total cost of production as it was extensively used in these areas to prevent environmental hazard.

Rural roads in Andhra Pradesh

CRRI has been entrusted the task of preparing a project report for the rural roads component of the Andhra Pradesh Economic Restructuring Project (APERP) funded by the World Bank. The study interalia includes the preparation of master plans, review of design standards, development of policy framework, identification of project scope. Three pilot districts were selected for the purpose to study the upgradation of a selected core network to all weather standards and building up of technical, institutional and financial capacity for sustainable maintenance and management of the core network. This study has proved that the core network identified by CRRI is cost effective and at the same time ensures 100% village accessibility.

Wind tunnel studies on structural models

SERC-M is now developing experimental techniques for testing of models of dynamically sensitive structures in the atmospheric boundary layer wind tunnel (BLWT) with the aim of improving the analytical tools for analysis of wind sensitive structures. Wind tunnel tests on 1:300 scale model of a coal storage shed without gable walls have been carried out. This enabled the optimisation of structure design to be done by a good bracing system connecting the frames in the front and rear.

Studies on vibration control of structures and foundations

SERC-M has taken up a project to study the dynamic characteristics of selected types of vibration isolators for developing standard criteria for analysis, design and evaluation of isolator supported machine foundations and investigate relative efficiency of base isolation techniques. A test facility for evaluating the dynamic stiffness and damping characteristics of vibration isolators under direct compression has been set up at the centre and trial tests have been carried out on a typical isolator having wide industrial application.

Finite element analysis of large structure using parallel processing

SERC-M has been working on development of parallel processing approaches for finite element analysis of large structures. Efficient mesh partitioning algorithms and a method of domain decompositions were developed for parallel processing. A portable Graphic User Interface (GUI) for the domain decomposition algorithms has been developed using X windows and Motif routines on workstation platforms. The expertise developed has enabled SERC-M to bag several grant-in-aid projects on specific aspects in the field.

Fatigue investigations of offshore structure

Corrosion fatigue behaviour of welded steel tubular joints of offshore structure has been experimentally investigated at SERC-M to formulate guidelines for fatigue-resistant design of offshore platform structures. The effect of cathodic protection on fatigue life of these joints was studied, both under constant amplitude and random loading. A life reduction factor by about 2 to 2.5 times was observed under free corrosion environment as compared to air environment. Adequate cathodic protection is found to help in restoring the in-air fatigue strength of tubular joints, both under constant amplitude and random loading conditions.

Creep damage and life assessment

A method for obtaining the oxidation rate constant under creep conditions has been suggested by NML. This is based on an analysis of the shape of the creep strain time plot. A new concept of a shape factor has been introduced for generating geometry independent master creep curves. The model has been validated with experimental data on Incone IX-750 and CrMoV steel. A finite Element Method based software has been developed to implement the model developed for specimen to the design of components.

Mining machinery components

In engineering components design apart material related factors like microstructural features, composition and engineering properties determines performance of a component. These parameters can be manipulated through appropriate metallurgical treatments, to ensure efficient working. RRL-Bhopal has taken up investigations on mining machinery components with a view to improve their life. Systematic metallurgical and tribological studies showed that life of indigenous shovel teeth could be enhanced to be at par with imported teeth.

Industrial roofing system using cold forming steel section

Use of Cold Forming Steel Section (CFSS) in structural construction, such as beams, columns etc. is yet to take off in any noticeable way in India. SERC-M took up a project to develop industrial roofing system using CFSS. Software was developed for determining the allowable axial load capacity and the bending strength of CFSS members as per IS: 8011975. Comparison of experimental result with applicable BS, AISI & IS codal provision brought to light the inadequacies of the present Indian code.

Technological achievements

Supersonic combustor development

DRDL, Hyderabad, is developing a hydrogen fuelled supersonic combustion ramjet for the hyperplane, which will be a fully reusable, single stage, hypersonic vehicle. As a part of this programme, NAL has developed the technology for the design of supersonic combustors. A direct connect supersonic combustor test facility, which is suitable for simulation of flight at six times the speed of sound and an altitude of 30 km altitude has been successfully set up and experimentally validated.

Development of powered hang glider

Probably for the first time in the world, a powered hang glider was flown with a rotary Wankel engine. The engine, an air-cooled 35 hp engine, was modified for this application in a project supported by AR&DB at NAL. NAL's flight activities involving the powered hang glider encourage the hope that the great potential of the Wankel engine may eventually be tapped.

Wide stall mining without stowing

Wide stall mining, an eco-friendly mining method without

stowing, has been developed by CMRI for optimal recovery of coal in developed pillars as well as for improvement in productivity and safety of workers for workings underneath delicate surfaces. The method was tried on experimental basis at Chirimiri mine of SECL for extraction of a 8.4m thick seam underneath a hill. The method is especially useful for regions where stowing materials are not available for packing of the mined-out areas.

Multiblend cement

CBRI has optimised four promising multiblend cement (MBC) formulations using portland cement clinkers and industrial by product wastes such as blast furnance slag, flyash and gypsum. These exhibit better strength, durability, impermeability and resistance to aggressive environments as compared to ordinary cements.

Natural rubber latex based cement concrete

SERC-M has developed a process for production of natural rubber latex based cement concrete (NR-LMCC), overcoming the problem of coagulation of the matrix which hinders the workability of concrete. The process has been utilised to develop mixed having higher strength, greater stiffness and more energy absorption compared to control concrete of M20 grade. The product exhibits quality of good adhesion to cementitious substrates, higher durability, impermeability to water, chlorides and carbon dioxide, resistance to salt water exposure and reduced drying shrinkage. The development is the subject matter of a patent application filed in India.

Epoxy concrete for machine bed

Epoxy concrete, a cold curing mixture of a reactable epoxy resin and hardener system (binder) and a carefully selected and graded aggregate system (filter), has potential in replacing cast iron and mild steel structural elements for machine tools. CMERI has taken up the development of epoxy concrete or epcon technology for manufacturing beds of grinding machines and other precision machine tools complete with inserts, including pre-machined metallic inserts, by in-situ casting methods. The technology has also been utilised for the manufacture of grinding machine beds with finished or semi-finished guideways, which can be moulded in with the main structure, bolted on to mould-in plates or cast with special formulation.

Corrosion resistance of fly ash cements

It has been reported that fly ash cement in general is less corrosion resistant compared to ordinary portland cement and hence large-scale blending of such cement in reinforced concrete construction is on the decline. CECRI has developed inhibitor admixture that will impart adequate corrosion resistance to flyash dust and facilitate its use in reinforced concrete.

Composition for quick Setting of cement

An inorganic chemical composition has been developed by CMRI for use in cement capsules to get instant grip, high strength and better performance compared to capsules available in the market. The know-how of the composition has been transferred to CIL. For effective use, the dry chemical is encapsulated in polythene capsules with closely spaced perforation. These capsules are immersed in water for few minutes before putting them into the holes. It has shown an anchorage strength of 2.5 to 3 tonnes after half-hour of installation.

Flyash for highway embankment construction

CRRI has successfully demonstrated the use of flyash for construction of highway embankments for the 6 to 9 meters high, 1.9 km long approach embankment for the Indo-Japan Friendship Bridge at Nizamuddin in New Delhi. Flyash has been used as a core material in floodzone area for the embankment.

Bio-energy for brick kilns

R&D efforts of CBRI to utilize high caloric value biomass as a partial or total substitute for coal & other fossil fuels for burning of bricks have yielded very encouraging results. Successful commercial trials utilizing agricultural by products and forest residues have been conducted at conventional Bull's trench kilns and other small scale intermittent kilns obtaining nearly 950 to 1000°C. The technique has been employed for commercial burning of bricks in Western UP, Haryana, Punjab and Gujarat where these bio-masses are available in plenty and also in other brick kilns situated far way from coal mine pits.

Cold forming of aluminium bicycle hubs

Cold forming is a process in which a near-net shape product with better mechanical properties can be achieved by forming a material at room temperature. CMERI has developed a suitable cold forming technology for aluminium alloy bicycle hub. The total hub was divided into two parts that were manufactured separately by cold forming process and were joined by friction welding to constitute the complete hub.

Improved iron removal for potable water

CMERI based on the inputs derived from evaluation and monitoring of iron removal plants installed under the RGNDWM has developed an improved version of iron removal plant. Better aeration by CMERI design features double aeration chambers and proper air flow; presettling chamber along with the settling chamber; optimum settling and filtration area that give significantly improved performance.

Decorticator for groundnut seeds

Decortification, a vital step in the production of edible oils from seeds is a candidate area requiring technological upgradation for optimisation of oil yield and quality. To bridge the existing gaps in technology. The MERADO,

Pune centre of CMERI under took the development of an efficient single roll decorticator for groundnut seeds. The design developed is versatile and enables decortication of groundnut as well as other seeds by changing the operating variables.

Remotely operated vehicle

CMERI has taken up the design and development of an upgraded version of a Remotely Operated Vehicle (ROV) to operate at a depth of 250 m, as an extension of the earlier sponsored programme of the DOD. The ROV will have application in marine geological survey, photography and collection of samples from the Exclusive Economic Zone.

Draft Tube (DT) Cone

BHEL Bhopal, manufactures hydroturbines of various capacities which presently employ DT cones imported from Japan and Russia. RRL-Bho developed and demonstrated seamless casting of acrylic polymer to make large thickness DT cones which also eliminated some of the design deficiencies. A prototype cone has been developed for BHEL for their model hydroturbine.

Lignin from paper mill effluents

India has a large number of pulp and paper mills based on agrowastes. These mills have capacity to produce 25-50 tons per day of paper, generate about 150 cubic meter of wastewater per ton of paper produced. The currently practiced processes do not have capability to separate the lignin and other components contributing to the high COD and BOD values to the effluent water.

NCL has developed a process for the treatment of the effluent water to separate the lignin. This process uses a material named as "ECONCL" developed at NCL (Indian Patent application filed). The effluent water when treated with ECONCL separates out the lignin and other Organic impurities as precipitate that settles down fast. The clarified water can be recycled in the pulp making plant. The process has been successfully demonstrated in the laboratory and pilot scale units at NCL.

Bioremediation for crude oil contaminated soil

RRL-Jorhat completed bench scale studies on 'bioremediation of crude oil contaminated soil of Borhola oil field' of ONGC. It lead to site characterisation and developing a bioremediation protocol for crude oil contaminated oil fields. The technique developed is expected to help restore the soil health of crude oil contaminated soils.

Eco-friendly coke-less cupola for Agra foundries

A tripartite agreement was signed between Tata-Korf, the Agra Iron Foundries Association (having nearly 250 foundries) and NNE for transfer of the coke-less cupola technology involving installation, commissioning, demonstration and diffusion in the Agra region. NML developed environment friendly coke-less cupola technology using liquid fuel or almost sulphur free natural gas will be engineered by Tata-Korf to commercial level for Agra foundries.

Food Processing

Scientific achievements

Lipase catalysed esterification

CFTRI has studied in detail the role of water of reaction and the micro-aqeous enzyme-water-solvent interphase on the esterification reaction catalysed by lipase. The studies score over usual chemical synthesis and other enzymatic process due to milder reaction conditions, low water environment, lesser concentrations of enzyme, less strenuous reaction conditions as compared to chemical synthesis and clean products. The investigations have generated information on these esterification equillibria useful in developing newer techniques for large scale applications. These studies have also resulted in the development of novel experimental designs for the synthesis of the esters on a bench scale level.

Spices as nutraceuticals

Spices and herbs are extensively used in Ayurvedic system of medicine. Investigations at CFTRI on dietary curcumin (from turmeric) and capsaicin (from chillies) have helped to establish the antiarthritic and antinflammatory properties of these spices as also explain the mechanisms by which these act on the pathological conditions. CFTRI has demonstrated the prophylactic and therapeutic effects of dietary curcumin and capsaicin in adjuvant induced arthritis model in rats. Studies showed that these spice principles delayed the onset of the disease, decreased inflammation of joints and reduced paw oedema in arthritic animals.

Biofumigants for the control of insect pests

CFTRI has discovered the potent biofumigant activity of a compound FPIC-CO01, present in foods conventionally used as a flavouring agent and also synthetically manufactured. FPIC-CO01 is listed as safe by the Flavour and Essence manufactures Association, USA. The insecticidal activity exhibited by the compound is seen to be the most potent as compared to other biofumigants being investigated elsewhere, thus having good potential for exploitation against mosquito mats, coils, vapourisers and use as a biofumigant for the protection of stored grain from insect infestation. The fumigant assumes importance in view of the phasing out of allethrin, phosphine and methyl bromide.

Technological achievements

Modified atmospheric packaging

Modified atmospheric packaging (MAP) wherein the atmosphere surrounding the commodity is rendered different from normal through manipulation of CO_2,O_2 and N_2 levels in suitable polymeric film packages of desired permeability is one of the effective methods for extending storage life of fruits. Active modification involves creating slight vacuum inside the package and replacing it with a desired mixture of gases to establish an optimum equilibrated modified atmosphere (EMA). The MAP offers potential for long distance transportation including export of commercially important fruits such as mango, banana, lichi, pomogranate and strawberry as well as important vegetables.

Technology protocols for mango export

Mango, considered the king of tropical fruits is a universal delicacy and has high potential for exports. CFTRI has developed specific pre-and post harvest technology packages for export of the famous alphonso and bangalpalli varieties of Indian mangoes by ship in reefer containers. The appropriate pre-harvest technology protocols include orchard management, treatments to control spoilage, optimum stage of maturity for harvest, desapping, grading, and washing followed by post-harvest dip treatments to minimise spoilage, ripening, low temperature storage in containers and packing in specially designed CFB boxes. The process capable of handling one tone mango per hour, helps in increasing shelf life of the produce to 35 days with desirable and acceptable ripening characteristics.

Dehydrated green pepper

Dehydrated green pepper (DGP) has a good potential for export. CFTRI has developed an improved process for dehydration of green pepper which avoids the use of chemicals for the retention of the green colour, a significant breakthrough in the technology development. Fresh tender green berries are subjected to high temperature in short time (HTST) treatment and then dried to a desired level under controlled conditions. The DGP thus obtained has a good flavour with a rehydration ratio of 1: 3, and a piperine content of about 5 %. A patent has been filed on this method for production of DGP.

Dehydration of meat

Dehydrated meat is a shelf-stable product and storable without refrigeration at ambient temperatures. It is a ready-to-use processed material which can be available at all times for preparation of meat dishes. CFTRI has developed a process for making the convenient ready-to-use meat and lends itself convenient to transportation.

Salt from the brines of Jambusar-quality improvement

Salt produced from subsoil brine available in Jambusar (Bharuch) is reported to be of inferior and inconsistent quality, CSMCRI developed a method which involved external additives and gives acceptable and consistent quality of salt.

National centre for food safety

The food related safety standards are now followed strictly by most of the countries. The health concerns for infants, children and elderly has made it necessary to put in place special regulations applicable to Infant and other foods. CFTRI under funding from DBT is setting up a National Centre for Food Safety. The Centre would house modern facilities for various food safety evaluations.

Information products

Scientific achievements

Mathematical models for assessment of stability

CMRI has developed mathematical comprehensive analysis models for assessment of stability criterion of wedges formed by four and five joint planes. The graphic software is used to determine rock pressure and optimum support design paratmeters of underground openings, tunnels and caverns. It also deals with the orientation of the drivage of excavation. The stability of abandoned mines, tunnels and caverns can also be assessed with the help of this package.

Benchmarking the best practice of Research and Technology Organisations (RTOs)

In the new environment of globalisation and liberalisation the RTOs are seeking to restructure but have little experience in organising their activities for the new environment. NISTADS after carefully studying RTOs the world over undertook a project aimed at addressing this question by setting up benchmarks and establishing a methodology. An information package has been developed on the methodology and best practices derived from the study.

Technological achievements

Software for fragment analysis

A fragment image analysis software package -FRAGALYST for post blast fragmentation has been developed by CMRI in collaboration with a private sector software company. This software accepts the digitized image of a pile of fragments and analyses the image for vital size and shape related information of visible fragments in the image. It offers variety of features, which help in visualizing scientific, statistical and geometric analysis of an image.

Software for electromagnetic design

NAL has developed a comprehensive software package, 'Aavrita' for EM design and analysis of radomes, both ground based and airborne. Aavrita aims at providing design solutions from the EM perspective incorporating variation in the material properties and the fabrication tolerances. Given a radome design, Aavrita is also capable of analysing it with respect to the EM performance parameters such as transmitted power, reflected power, voltage standing wave ratio (VSWR), insertion phase delay (IPD) etc.

Software for cathodic protection in off-shore platforms

The software is the first of its kind in India and has been developed for ONGC, subsequent to denial of the international software from the Norwegian consortium. Offshore platforms are expensive metallic structures for oil & gas exploration, the longivity of these structures thus depends critically on the extent of cathodic protection provided to them. CECRI has developed an highly useful indigenous software called CPSEA++ which facilitates early recognition of corrosion and areas prone to corrosion, thereby providing timely protection of off-shore structures.

Software for the analysis of deflection data

Under a joint study with C-MMACS, CRRI has developed a Mathematical Model for Multilayer Road System, Types prevalent in India and a software analysis of Falling Weight Deflectometer deflection data. Validation of the software is being carried out.

Engineering database on landslides

CRRI has developed a user friendly engineering database on landslides (EDBLSD) comprising all important factors influencing landslides and the associated impacts. The database would be useful towards developing national policies on mitigation and management of landslides and also assist highway engineers working on hilly regions in preparing at operational strategic plans.

Mufti-media database creation

INSDOC has been making endeavours to develop expertise in the area of multimedia databases. It has developed the following multi-media products:

a) *Multi media Encyclopedia on Carnatic Music:* The database is of hypermedia documents which are linked to each other through hyperlinks. It has been authored in ICON AUTHOR software, provides detailed information in the form of text, picture or sound on the various aspects of Carnatic music.

b) *Multi media Photo I-card Preparation:* INSDOC has developed a high efficiency system for the preparation which enables online delivery of photo I-cards. It continued the preparation of photo I-cards for electors of 50 assembly constituencies in the National Capital Territory of Delhi.

CD-ROM activities

INSDOC has published two databases on CD-ROM using in house facilities these are:

a) National Union Catalogue of Scientific Serials in India (NUCSSI) Database: It is a valuable user friendly menu-driven retrieval information product which helps in locating the availability of S&T serials in the country. The database covers nearly two lakh holdings in over 400 S&T libraries in the country.

b) Indian Patents (INPAT) Database can be searched by different parameters. It contains nearly 50,000 records on patents granted in India from 1972 to December 1997.

Publication of research journals

NISCOM, continued the publication of the thirteen research journals covering all the major disciplines of science. In all nearly 1400 papers were published in these journals during the year. Some Special issues of these journals brought out during the year were on:

a) Organic Synthesis-Growing Interface with Adjacent Sciences proceedings of an Indo-German Symposium (Indian Journal of Chemistry, Sections A&B June, 1997);

b) Condensed matter Physics (Indian Journal of Pure and Applied Physics, November 1997) ;

c) Role of Eukaryotic Cell Surface Macromolecules (Indian Journal of Biochemistry and Biophysics, February & April 1998 combined issue);

d) Satellite Oceanographic Modelling (Indian Journal of Marine Sciences, march 1998);

e) Recent Advances in Technical Textiles (Indian Journal of Fibre and Textile Research, December 1997) ;

f) The publication of the Chinese editions of Indian Journal of Chemistry, Sections A&B was continued in collaboration with the Shanghai World Publishing Corporation, Shanghai.

Special publications

NISCOM published two reference proceedings, viz; Advances in High Pressure Research in Condensed Matter Physics, Proceedings of International Conference on Condensed matter under High. Pressure held at BARC during Nov. 1996, the Physics of Disordered Materials, Proceedings of the International Conference held at Jaipur in January 1997. All the twenty-four issues of the fortnightly newsletter CSIR News for the year were published on schedule.

Popularisation of science

The Golden Jubilee series of popular science books initiated at NISOM during 1992 have been in great demand, a new title brought out was on 'Holography' by M.G. Joshi. In the Sci-Fun Series of books targeted for children in the age group of 8-10, a new title on 'Bubble Bubble by HS Ray was published and the manuscripts of two other books, 'Strange Plants' by Parul Sheth and 'Deserts' by Vineeta Singhal, are press ready. Besides this two lavishly illustrated books 'How?' and 'Why?' each containing 100 mind boggling questions (with their answers) in was released under the Q-Series.

Documentation centre for RGNDWM

INSDOC has been approached by Rajiv Gandhi National Drinking Water Mission (RGNDWM) for establishment of its Documentation and Information Centre on a turn key basis. The project phase involving setting up of infrastructural facilities is nearing completion which will be followed by an operational phase of one year. The resource collection for the centre is being built up concurrently. The first issue of the quarterly R&D newsletter entitled "MISSION NVATS AN" has been published. The centre is scheduled to be inaugurated shortly.

Electoral roll database

INSDOC was assigned by Chief Electoral Officer (CEO), Delhi a project on computerisation of electoral rolls of the National Capital Territory of Delhi. The work involved creation of a database of nearly 45 lakh electors of 40 Assembly constituencies in English and Hindi. The software has been developed in 'Windows' and database design provides improved storage efficiency by introducing dictionary concept. It facilitates conversion of English data into Hindi automatically. The database will simplify the process of updating electoral rolls and bring about overall improvement in the management of electoral rolls data.

Material sciences and technology

Scientific achievements

RF-SQUID effect in borocarbide superconductors

NPL has observed, for the first time, rf-SQUID effect due to natural grain boundary weak links in a bulk sample of YNi_2B_2C superconductor at 4.2 K, confirming that the superconducting grains are coupled at the grain boundaries through Josephson effect.

Thermal modelling of DC continuous casting

NML has developed an efficient numerical simulation method for the steady-state Direct-Chill continuous casting of aluminium-magnesium (AI-Mg) alloy cylindrical ingots, results from which show excellent agreement with the published experimental data.

Foaming behaviour of FeO in slags during reduction

RRL-Bhu conducted a number of experiments in a plasma reactor of 50 kW capacity to investigate the influence of

FeO content in slag on the foaming taking place in hearth portion of the blast furnace in steel making. It was seen that the maximum foam height increased with decrease of temperature, initial FeO content of slag and initial slag height.

Technological achievements

High temperature superconducting wires/tapes and tube conductors

Keeping the possibility of use of high temperature superconductors as current carrying conductor in mind, NPL has been developing technology for fabrication of silver clad superconducting wires using high temperature superconducting BPSCCO conductors on:

a) Fabrication of long length silver clad BPSCCO mono-filamentary;

b) Fabrication of multi-filamentary silver clad BPSCCO tapes and;

c) Fabrication of high current tube conductors.

It appears that high current leads featuring rods or tubes would be the first applications of ceramic superconductors in electrical power engineering as they offer a major advantage of reduction of heat load at 41K by more than a factor of 10 with a current of 500-1000 A for various applications. NPL has prepared 10,20 and 43 cms long tube conductors capable of carrying more than 120-200 A at 771K in the superconducting state. These can be used as current leads for conventional superconducting magnets, particularly suitable for operation with cryo-coolers.

Carbon ore epoxy prepregs

By virtue of the numerous advantages they offer prepregs are the most popular 'building blocks' in composite product development. Currently most prepregs used in India are imported. NAL, with support from TIFAC and ADA has developed aerospace grade carbon fibre prepregs know how which has been transferred to IPCL, Vadodara.

Ultra low expansion transparent glass-ceramic

Ultra low expansion transparent glass-ceramic is a strategic material used as a mirror substrate mount for astronomical telescopes, reflector in radiometer of satellites and as standard reference material for dimension control in engineering industry. CGCRI carried out extensive work on the development of the ceramic (equivalent to 'ZERODUR') and has been successful in producing 5 kg of the strategic material and moulded glass blanks of different sizes. Scale up to a 100 litre melting capacity plant is now contemplated.

Radiation Shielding Windows (RSW) glass

CGCRI has been successful in developing a high density (>=5.0 g/cm^3) RSW glass (both unstabilised and Ce-stabilized in lab-scale (2kg) under the sponsorship of Board of Research in Nuclear Sciences (BRNS), Department of Atomic Energy (DAE). Efforts are on to upscale the melting parameters for the preparation of large size (150×150×100 mm) blanks for further evaluation.

Flotation column for industrial applications

A 75mm diameter automated flotation column designed by NML Madras Centre was fabricated and supplied to National Mineral Development Corporation Ltd., Hyderabad. The column incorporates many salient features like precise feed/discharge controls and level controls and is highly automated.

Encouraged by the success and the excellent metallurgical results obtained using this column, NML recently designed and developed a semi-commercial column of 50 mm, diameter with a capacity to treat 2-4 tonnes of ores per hour. This column has complete instrumentation for level control, wash water control, automatic sampling etc. It incorporates a special sparger designed and developed at the Centre. The column has been successfully tested for Bharat Gold Mines Ltd., at

Kolar Goldfields for their gold ores and for Gujarat Mineral Development Corporation, at Kadipani for fluorspar.

Tiles from ferro-chrome and other industrial wastes

The mixing and grinding for various compositions were chosen and carried out in pot mill to get the desired fineness and the parameters were optimised. The tiles were then fired in an electric furnace at a sintering temperature in the range of 1050-1150°C. The properties of these tiles were evaluated with reference to the European Nation (EN) Standards of ceramic tiles and were found to confirm to the standards in most aspects.

Improvement in efficiency of ferro-chromium, process

NML has developed a thermochemical model of the production of FeCr in the Submerged Arc Furnace to predict the quantity of metal that could be produced. An excellent correlation was observed between the quantity predicted by the model and the amount actually produced in a 150 TPA plant. It is estimated that an industrial unit could secure about Rs. 100 lakh per annum from productivity improvement by implementing the process modifications arising from the model.

Masonry cement from industrial wastes

CBRI has taken up work on utilising mining and industrial wastes for production of masonry cement. Performance evaluation of a number of preliminary mixes of desired fineness prepared by varying proportions of wastes as binary and tertiary systems was done and mix proportions optimised with respect to percentage wastes. The product is cheaper than portland cement and found to be equally good for plastering and mortar purposes.

Transmittance standards for the infrared

Infrared radiation standards are not readily available from any of the standards laboratories in the world. The currently available standards provided by the National Institute of Standards & Technology (NIST), USA, operate in the uv, visible, and near infrared spectral region up to 2.5 m only. Now, NIST has established wavelength scale for the calibration of FTIR instruments. NPL has worked on the development transmittance standards at normal as well as oblique angles (10 to 70 degree) of incidence in the infrared (2.5 to 25 m) spectral region. The materials employed are silicon germanium, potassium bromide, zinc sulphide, zinc selenide and calcium fluoride. The transmittance/reflectance values of these standards have been intercompared with those measured at NIST and have been found to be in good agreement. These standards are used for the calibration of infrared spectrophotometers/radiometers which are an important tool for analysing the product quality in various industries i.e. chemical, pharmaceutical, food, tobacco etc. and for the evaluation of the performance of infrared scanners, night vision, thermo-vision and remote sensing systems by measuring the true transmittance of their window materials and filters.

Physical sciences and earth resources

Scientific achievements

Modelling of biogeochemical cycles of the Indian ocean

The study of biogeochemical cycles of the Indian Ocean are important for the estimation of carbon flux and marine fishery potential. A nonlinear dynamical system model developed by C-MMAC consisting of twenty seven parameters has been applied to the Indian Ocean. The model includes the effect of upwelling velocity, photosynthetically active radiation, nonlinear closure terms and grazing threshold. The model tuning is being carried out to capture the chlorophyll seasonal variation in the upper ocean, as obtained from CZCS data.

Crustal deformation using global positioning system

C-MMACS analysed the Global Positioning System

measurements data collected in the last 3 years, to estimate the convergence rate of the observation points in North India with respect to observation point in IISc to assess the stability of the South Indian peninsula using the International GPS Service (IGS) estimated orbits and pole parameters and International Terrestrial Reference Frame (ITRF 96). The results suggest that the point in Delhi has not moved much with respect to Bangalore in the last two and half years, implying that the Indian plate between Delhi and Bangalore is relatively stable. However two points in Garhwal Himalaya, one is Chamba (CHAM) just north of Main Boundary thrust and the Sukhi (SUKI) point north of Chamba, are converging towards the Indian plate at the rate of 14 rum and 18 mm/ per year. Analysis of four South Indian points with respect to Bangalore point yielded average linear strain rate of 0.001 microstrain/year, establishing the stability of South Indian peninsula and least possibility of occurrence of big earthquakes. There is also an indication of volumetric strain of the South Indian peninsula.

Insitu stress measurement

Insitu stress measurements have been carried out by NGRI upto ~600m depth in a very small diameter core-drilled borehole in the meizoseismal area of Latur earthquake for the first time in the world using a miniaturized hydroffacture packer assembly. The results demonstrate that the near-surface principal horizontal stresses are higher than the overburden pressure, indicating that they are of tectonic origin.

Earthquake studies

NGRI carried out a number of earthquake studies, leading to significant findings, some of these are given here under:

a) At Koyna the 3-13 velocity image suggests that this zone is marked by high velocity in upper crust as well as in deep lithosphere. Hypocentral locations revealed two NNE-SSW trending active faults at a depths of 11 km. The moderate earthquakes were found to nucleate near the surface, but propagating northward and downward, within planar rupture areas of 70-80sq. km. The depth range of 0-1 and 5-11 km were found to give higher magnitude and higher stress drop events.

b) At Jabalpur study of fault plane solution, isoseismals and aftershocks indicates overthrusting of southern block, of the ENE-WSW trending south Narmada fault at a depth of 35 km. The fault length is estimated to be about 5.7 km. Gravity profiles across epicentral zone of this earthquake delineated a horst structure between north and south Narmada faults which is related to the epicentre. Inferred structure across the Narmada-Son lineament obtained from MT studies could be related to seismogenic fault related to Jabalpur earthquake.

c) At Latur site amplification and coda Q_c attenuation evaluated by using after shock digital data showed that the maximum amplitude of site amplification was at villages around Killari. The fault length for the Latur earthquake is found to he 4.8 km. Teleseismic broadband data of Latur and Jabalpur earthquakes reveals that for these earthquakes the corner frequency estimate are relatively consistent. The Latur earthquakes indicates a stress drop and apparent stress which are 5 times more compared to the Jabalpur earthquake.

Oceanographic studies

i) Coastal studies

a) Under the Coastal Ocean Monitoring and Prediction System (COMAPS) extensive chemical and biological observations were made by NIO during pre and post monsoon seasons along Ratnagiri-Mangalore coastal stretch. The studies indicated that the region is free from contamination. Higher values of standing stock and densities of zooplankton were observed during premonsoon than postmonsoon season.

b) Cycling of combined nitrogen in sediment and water column of mangroves were studied. It was observed that nitrate dominated in the water column while nitrate as well as ammonium occurred in high concentrations in the sediments. Experiments on uptake and assimilation of nitrogenous nutrients by phytoplankton of sediment and water column indicated that ammonium was the most preferred nutrient to be taken up by the autotrophs with high specific rates in the month of May.

c) Studies on littoral drift and sink along the Indian coast indicated an active removal of sediments in the Gulf of Kachchh, Gulf of Khambhat, Gulf of Mannar, Palk Bay and Sandheads. Strong currents and wave energy concentrations are the causative factors resulting in coastal erosion.

d) Hydrographic data collected during the pre and post southwest monsoon seasons in Gauthami Godavari estuary were utilised to estimate residual fluxes of water salt and vertical diffusivity. The residual flux of salt due to tidal pumping appears to be the main factor controlling the salt balance of the estuary.

ii) Offshore processes

a) Magnetic survey along a transect running from 1^0S, 81^0 24′E to 7^0N, 87^0 WE has led to the identification of a cretaceous Magnetic Quiet Zone (CMQ) in the distal Bengal Fan. This has established a continuous evolutionary record of the Bay of Bengal since India's break up from the eastern Gondwana continent. Bathymetric and magnetic studies in the distal Bengal Fan reveal the presence of -seamounts, which are possible locations of polymetallic encrustations.

b) Under the Joint Global Ocean Flux Study (JGOFS India) programme, the spatial and temporal variability in air-sea fluxes of carbon dioxide was studied and found that higher biological production results in higher respiration rates. The surface waters of the central Arabian Sea are supersaturated, with respect to pCO_2 in atmosphere.

c) High resolution seismic reflection profiting along the western continental margin of India revealed the presence of characteristic acoustic maskings in the form of wipeouts, reflector terminations and seeps in the inner shelf. These maskings are considered to be methane-rich. Seismic profiles also revealed the presence of bottom simulating reflectors (BSRs) in the mid-lower slope-rise regions, presumably suggesting the presence of gas hydrates.

Central Indian ocean basin studies

In the first phase programme on Environmental impact Assessment at NIO for nodule mining, studies for evaluating the baseline (undisturbed) conditions have been completed in the test and reference areas. Wailed analyses of the seafloor features, nodule distribution, bathymetry, sediment characteristics and composition, as well as macro, meiobenthic and micro-biological assemblages, have been carried out to understand the present status of the benthic environment. In the second phase, a simulated "Disturbance" was conducted at a pre-selected test site.

The result showed that the changes, were the greatest within the disturbance zone, whereas the resedimentation from the plume generated by the disturber, was concentrated mainly in the southern and southwestern directions of the zone, which corresponds to the mean direction of currents during that period.

Technological achievements

Green house gave inventory

The NPL in association with other sister CSIR laboratories has developed the greenhouse gas inventory (GHG) for India since 1991. The 1998 report from NPL is the most comprehensive report to dates. The base-year considered for calculations in this report is 1990. The various sectors for which emission estimates have been made are: (i) Energy which includes emissions from Industry and Transport; (ii) the Agriculture sector (rice paddy fields and enteric fermentation from animals and manure, emissions due to burning of agricultural crop residue and emissions from Wetlands); (iii) Land use changes and forestry sector includes emissions from grassland conversion, change in forests and other woody biomass stock, abandonment of managed lands and finally the net emission from forestry and land use sector; (iv) the Waste sector includes emissions from municipal land filled areas and area in which fruit and vegetable waste are dumped. (v) waste water emissions.

Laser heterodyne system in Antartica

A highly sophisticated and High-Tech laser heterodyne system using a tunable CO_2 laser as a local oscillator and sun as a source with one GHz acousto-optic spectrometer (AOS) as back end has been designed and developed at NPL. I was deployed at Maitri station (70^0 46' S, $11^0$44'E) in Antarctica during 161 Indian Scientific Antarctica expedition (1996-97) to measure the vertical profiles of minor constituents in the stratosphere and troposphere.

The observations for ozone line profiles were continued during 1997-98 on all clear blue sky/ cloudless sunny days. The ozone line profiled thus obtained are in turn used to get vertical height profiles of ozone using inversion technique developed again at NPL for Antarctic conditions. This is the firm time that this system has been deployed for Antarctic winter time and data were collected successfully during spring i.e, September-October to study ozone bole.

Identification of deep seated weak zones

Multi-parametric geophysical studies by NGRI in thick sand covered areas of the Thar desert near Jaisalmer have succeeded in identifying deep seated weak zones, oriented broadly in the NNW-SSE and NE direction. These zones, that have played a significant role in the emplacement of dykes during earlier magnetic episodes, are important for assessing groundwater circulation.

Gravity anomaly map

Based on zero free air values, NGRI prepared a new gravity anomaly map for South India. This map can be directly interpreted in terms of subsurface mass in homogeneities and has brought into focus new anomalies which were not identified earlier from the Bouguer anomaly map due to negative bias.

Comparative assessment of clean coal technologies

CFRI commissioned an exercise to assess the relative merits of thermally efficient technologies for coal conversion to assess their applicability for Indian coals using ASPEN simulator. Eight technologies, four based on gasification and four based on combustion including conventional pulverized coal system were chosen for the study. Conversion efficiency as a function of varying quality of coal with respect to pure coal heat value and ash content and unit cost of power generation in relation to pulverized coal combustion has been worked out.

Societal and huuman welfare

Scientific achievements

Neuroendocrine regulation of silk Protein biosynthesis

The neurosecretory system of the Muga silkworm with particular emphasis of neurosecretory cells (NEC) at different regions of the brain and their positional arrangements according to the age of the silkworm was studied at RRL-Jorhat. The ultrastructure of the silk gland and brain during developmental stages showed qualitative and quantitative variations in their secretory products which clearly suggests direct control of the neuroendocrine system over silk gland development and silk protein biosynthesis.

Technological achievements

Leather Technology (LTM)

LTM made a tangible impact on the national scenario, through nearly 160 activities initiated in 17 States, of these 90 activities were completed. The highlights of achievements during the year are as follows:

a) Twelve carcass utilisation benefiting 300 families.

b) Field implementation viz. enzyme assisted dehairing, chrome recovery/ reuse, chrome management etc. were carried out in several locations.

c) A demonstration common effluent treatment plant (CETP) was commissioned at Madhavaram. Process control systems and cleaner tannery wet operations were demonstrated at four tanneries in UP and Haryana.

d) Human resource development activities viz. Programmes for artisanal development, training of shop floor management personnel for leather industry, training of trainers, training of women were carried out at several locations. Twenty cobblers from Chennai and Guntur were trained in modern methods of foot ware manufacture. Two hundred artisans from Athani have been trained in improved tanning of sole leather.

Rehabilitation of tanners in Tamil Nadu

The project aptly named 'Operation Greenstar' was luanched on a warfooting as a tripartite arrangement between CLRI, NEERI and AISHTMA. Each of the partners was assigned a designated role and responsibility; CLRI for technology for inplant control, NEERI for end of the pipe treatment and AISHTMA for implementation of the technology.

CLRI carried out an intensive survey of nearly 500 tanneries to identify and establish process information and operational data of each tannery. As a result 36 cluster groups were formed for implementation of the technology intervention packages comprising green technologies for beam-house operations, clearner tanning techniques and effluent treatment systems. NEERI carried out surveys on estimation of quantity and characteristics of the Waste Waters, based on which designs of new and redesign of existing common effluent treatment plants (CETPs) was undertaken to enable cenfermance with satutory norms. The design involved high rate transpiration & sludge management system. This enabled about 500 tanneries to be rehabilitated and made up for the loss of employment of the disadvantaged section of the society.

Value added products from tannery wastes

Tannery fleshings and chicken intestines, the two major wastes from tannery and poultry industries pose disposal problems. CLRI has studied the enzymatic hydrolysis of tannery fleshings using chicken intestine protease. The protein hydrolysate obtained could be used in poultry or fish feed formulations. In investigations on chicken intestines as a source of proteolytic and autolytic enzymes for hydrolysis of tannery fleshings, it was seen that about 75% of the total protease activity of the chicken intestines was in the mucosal layer.

Ethnobotanical investigations of Kangra Valley in Himachal Pradesh
NBRI carried out an extensive ethnobotanical investigation in Kangra valley. It has provided new knowledge on the traditional uses of several plant species which can be utilized in tribal development programmes. The inventory provides very useful data for establishing plant based cottage industries in the tribal tracts, especially for herbal drugs, food processing, fibre products and gum resin etc.

Improvement in rose oil distillation unit
IHBT improved upon an existing rose oil distillation unit (400kg capacity per batch) by integrating a compatible cohobation column designed by it with the oil distillation unit resulting in 30% increase in oil recovery.

Mechanisation of tea plucking
IHBT has standardised the mechanical plucking of china hybrid tea by machines keeping in view the two leaves and a bud plucking standard. This will greatly help the tea industry in Himachal Pradesh, which is currently facing the problem of labour shortage.

New propagation technology for tea
IHBT has succeeded in propagation of tea by 4 to 8 node cuttings as against conventional method of single node cutting by treating the node cuttings with different auxins and phenols resulting in 85-90% success in rooting and transfer to field within 9 months as against conventional methods needing nearly 2 years.

Banana fibre
RRL, Jorhat undertook study on the utilisation of wild banana plants for producing fibres and other useful materials. The main objective was to develop an appropriate technology to extract fibres from the sheaths of banana plants and then convert the fibres into twines and fabrics in conventional jute processing machinery for making eco-friendly products. Based on this work the Government of Sri Lanka has requested RRL, Jorhat to

extend technical assistance to develop industries based on banana fibre in Sri Lanka and to impart training to Sri Lankan entrepreneurs.

Fresh water prawn cultivars

The suitability of freshwater prawn Macrobrachium rosenbergii for commercial production- was tested by NIO with minor modifications of the hatchery for rearing the larvae. Water quality management, feed formulation and feeding schedule for different larval stages and maintenance of hygiene in the hatchery are the factors which control the growth of larvae. Commercial production of larvae with this technique was achieved.

Habilitation at the mentally challenged people

NISTADS conceived and executed a field experiment called SAKSHAM (meaning empowered or enabling) for habilitating the mentally challenged adults to become partially/fully economically independent. A reconnaissance study was conducted by NISTADS to understand the actual condition of the mentally challenged adult after they leave the special schools or vocational centres followed by another study of employing appropriate select technologies which they could pursue as a vocational career to move on the path of economic independence. The technology of mushroom cultivation was selected for field testing the concept. Though mushroom cultivation technology is well known, application of this environment sensitive technology by a group of mentally challenged people made the experiment unique. Ibis was a departure from routine repetitive tasks used for training such people. It proved that mentally challenged were capable of performing more complex functions than is usually believed. The Project has since been selected as on the innovative projects having societal impact potential by Third World Network of Scientific Organisations (TWNSO), Trieste, and the United Nations Development Programme (UNDP) of sharing of experience among developing countries.

Floricultuure industry in H.P.

Floriculture was most non-existing in Himachal Pradesh (HP) a decade back. Arising from the training imparted to 150 growers of HP by IHBT on commercial floriculture sponsored by the Govt. of Hp, DRDA and HIMCON. 150 ha have been brought under commercial floriculture.